The Lost Keys of Masonry

The Legend of Hiram Abiff

—— By ——

Manly Hall

Author of Occult Masonry, The Sacred
Magic of the Qabbalah, Initiates
of the Flame, The Ways of the
Lonely Ones, Etc.

Proem by Reynold E. Blight, 33°
Illustrated by J. Augustus Knapp, 32°

SECOND EDITION

Hall Publishing Company
Los Angeles
1924

G. RAYMOND BROWN PRINTING COMPANY

O. G. M. H. A. B.
The Spirit of Masonry.
Within all the swirling substances of
nature, the martyred builder of the
Masonic legend lies buried, awaiting
the day of liberation, when his faithful
sons shall free him for his cosmic labor.

In this picture Hiram represents the spirit of universal vitality. This is the original meaning of the allegory and is the reason why the Masonic initiation is both individually and eternally true. -:-

Dedicated to
The Ancient Order of Free and
Accepted Masons

PROEM

By Reynold E. Blight
33° K. T.

Reality forever eludes us. Infinity mocks our puny efforts to imprison it in definition and dogma. Our most splendid realizations are only adumbrations of the Light. In his endeavors, man is but a mollusk seeking to encompass the ocean.

Yet man may not cease his struggle to find God. There is a yearning at the soul of him that will not let him rest, an urge that compels him to attempt the impossible, to attain the unattainable. He lifts feeble hands to grasp the stars and despite a million years of failure and millenniums of disappointment, the soul of man springs heavenward with even greater avidity than when the race was young.

He pursues, even though the flying ideal eternally slips from his embrace. Even though he never clasps the goddess of his dreams, he refuses to believe that she is a phantom. To him she is the only reality. He reaches upward and will not be content until the sword of Orion is in his hands, and glorious Arcturus gleams from his breast.

3

Man is Parsifal searching for the Sacred Cup; Sir Launfal adventuring for the Holy Grail. Life is a divine adventure, a splendid quest.

Language fails. Words are mere cyphers, and who can read the riddle? These words we use, what are they but vain shadows of form and sense? We strive to clothe our highest thought with verbal trappings that our brother may see and understand; and when we would describe a saint he sees a demon; when we would present a wise man he beholds a fool. "Fie upon you," he cries; "thou, too, art a fool."

So wisdom drapes her truth with symbolism, and covers her insight with allegory. Creeds, rituals, poems are parables and symbols. The ignorant take them literally and build for themselves prison houses of words and with bitter speech and bitterer taunt denounce those who will not join them in the dungeon. Before the rapt vision of the seer, dogma and ceremony, legend and trope dissolve and fade, and he sees behind the fact the truth, behind the symbol the Reality.

Through the shadow shines ever the Perfect Light.

What is a Mason? He is a man who in his heart has been duly and truly prepared, has been found worthy and well qualified, has been admitted to the fraternity of builders, been invested with certain passwords and signs by which he may be enabled to work and receive wages as a Master Mason, and travel in foreign lands in search of that which was lost—The Word.

Down through the misty vistas of the ages rings a clarion declaration and although the very heavens echo to the reverberations, but few hear and fewer understand: "In the beginning was the Word and the Word was with God and the Word was God."

Here then is the eternal paradox. The Word is lost, yet it is ever with us. The light that illumines the distant horizon shines in our hearts. "Thou would'st not seek me hadst thou not found me." We travel afar only to find that which we hunger for at home.

And as Victor Hugo says: "The thirst for the Infinite proves infinity."

That we seek lives in our souls.

This, the unspeakable truth, the unutterable perfection, the author has set before us in these pages. Not a Mason himself, he has read the deeper meaning of the ritual. Not having assumed the formal obligations, he calls upon all mankind to enter into the holy of holies. Not initiated into the physical craft, he declares the secret doctrine that all may hear.

With vivid allegory and profound philosophical disquisition he expounds the sublime teachings of Free Masonry, older than all religions, as universal as human aspiration.

It is well. Blessed are the eyes that see, and the ears that hear, and the heart that understands.

FOREWORD
TO THE SECOND EDITION

The kindly attitude with which the first edition of this work was received has prompted the author to enlarge it and to send it forth again, trusting that it may assist in clearing up some of the mysteries which have long shrouded Masonry's place in the spiritual, ethical, and scientific world.

CONTENTS

ILLUSTRATIONS

INTRODUCTION

I

MASONRY is essentially a religious order. Most of its legends and allegories are of a sacred nature. Much of Masonry is woven into the structure of Christianity. We have learned to consider our own religion as the only inspired one, and this probably accounts for a great many of the misunderstandings existing in the world today concerning the place occupied by Masonry in the spiritual ethics of our race. A religion is a divinely inspired code of morals. A religious person is one inspired to nobler living by this code. He is identified by the code which is his source of illumination. Thus we may say that a Christian is one who receives his spiritual ideals of right and wrong from the message of the Christ, while a Buddhist is one who molds his life into the archetype of moral status given by the great Gautama, or one of the other Buddhas. All doctrines which seek to unfold and preserve that invisible spark in man which he has named *Spirit*, are said to be spiritual. Those which ignore this invisible element and concentrate entirely upon the visible are said to be material. There is in religion a wonderful place of balance—where the materialist and spiritist meet on the plane of logic and reason. Science and theology are two ends of a single truth, but the world will never receive the full benefit of their investigations until they have made peace with each other, and labor hand in hand for the accomplishment of the great work—the liberation of spirit and intelligence from the three-dimentional graves of ignorance, superstition, and fear.

That which gives man a knowledge of himself can be inspired only by the self—and God is the self in all things. In truth, He is the inspiration and the thing inspired. It has been stated in Scripture that God was the Word and that the Word was made flesh. Man's task now is to make flesh reflect the glory of that Word, which is within the soul of himself. It is this task which has created the need of religion—not one faith alone, but many creeds, each searching in its own way: each meeting the needs of individual people: each emphasizing one point above all the others.

Twelve Fellow Craftsmen are exploring the four points of the compass. Are not these twelve the twelve great world religions, each seeking in its own way for that which was lost in the ages past, and the quest of which is the birthright of man? Is not the quest for Reality in a world of illusions the task for which each comes into the world? We are here to gain balance in a sphere of unbalance; to find rest in a restless thing; to unveil illusion; and to slay the dragon of our own animal natures. As David, King of Israel, gave to the hands of his son Solomon the task he could not accomplish, so each generation gives to the next the work of building the temple, or rather, rebuilding the dwelling of the Lord, which is on the Mount Moriah.

Truth is not lost, yet it must be sought for and found. Reality is ever-present—dimensionless, yet all-prevailing. Man—creature of attitudes and desires, and servant of impressions and opinions —cannot, with the wandering unbalance of an untutored mind, learn to know that which he himself does not possess. As man attains a quality, he discovers that quality, and recognizes about him the thing newborn within himself. Man is born with eyes, yet it is only after long years of sorrow that he learns to see clearly and in harmony with the plan. He is born with senses, but it is only after long experience and fruitless strivings that he brings these senses to the temple and lays them as offerings upon the altar of the great Father, who alone does all things well and with understanding. Man is, in truth, born in the sin of ignorance, but with a capacity for understand·

ing. He has a mind capable of wisdom, a heart capable of feeling, and a hand strong for the great work in life—truing the rough ashler into the perfect stone.

What more can any creature ask for than an opportunity, a chance to prove the thing he is, the dream that inspires him, the vision that leads him on? We have no right to ask for wisdom. In whose name do we beg for understanding? By what authority do we demand happiness? None of these things is the birthright of any creature; yet all may have them, if they will cultivate within themselves the thing that they desire. There is no need of asking, nor does any Deity bow down to give man these things that he desires. Man is given, by nature, a gift, and that gift is the privilege of labor. Through labor he learns all things.

Religions are groups of people, gathered together in the labor of learning. The world is a school. We are here to learn, and being here proves our need of instruction. Every living creature is struggling to break the strangling bonds of limitation—that pressing narrowness which destroys vision and leaves the life without an ideal. Every soul is engaged in a great work —the labor of personal liberation from the ruts of ignorance. The world is a great prison: its bars are the Unknown. And each is a prisoner, until

16

Three murderers slay the spirit of life in man: perverted thoughts, uncurbed emotions, and destructive actions. These three together abuse and pervert energy and bring down the Temple of Creation in a ruin about their own heads.   -:-   -:-   -:-   -:-

*In the Ancient Mysteries a woman was used to sym-
bolize the emotional nature of man, as emotional ex-
cess is one of the murderers of universal energy. A
woman was used in the Egyptian Rites. This has
been discontinued, but it is nevertheless correct.* -:-

at last he earns the right to tear these bars from their moldering sockets, and pass, illuminated and inspired, into the darkness, which becomes lighted by that presence. All peoples of the world seek the temple where God dwells, where the spirit of the great Truth illuminates the shadows of human ignorance, but they know not which way to turn, nor where this temple is. The mist of dogma surrounds them. Ages of thoughtlessness bind them in. Limitation weakens them and inhibits their footsteps. They wander in darkness seeking light, ever failing to realize that the light is in the heart of the darkness.

To a few who have found Him, God reveals Himself. These, in turn, reveal Him to man, striving to tell ignorance the message of wisdom. But seldom does man understand the mystery that has been unveiled. He tries weakly to follow in the steps of those who have attained, but all too often finds the path more difficult than he even dreamed. So he kneels in prayer before the mountain he cannot climb, and from the top of which gleams forth the light, which he is not strong enough to reach, nor wise enough to comprehend. He lives the law as he knows it, always fearing in the depth of himself that he has not read aright the flaming letters in the sky, and that in living the letter of the Law he has murdered out the spirit. Man bows humbly to the Unknown, peopling the shadows of his own ignorance with saints and saviors, ghosts and specters, gods and demons. Ignorance fears all things, and falls, terror-stricken, before the passing wind. Superstition stands as the monument to ignorance, and before it kneel those who are realizing their own weakness; who see in all things the strength they do not possess; who give to sticks and stones the power to bruise them; who change the beauties of nature into the dwelling places of ghouls and ogres. Wisdom fears no thing, but still bows humbly to its own source. While superstition hates all things, wisdom, with its deeper understanding, loves all things, for it has seen the beauty, the tenderness, and the sweetness which underlie Life's mystery.

Life is the span of time appointed for accomplishment. Every fleeting moment is an opportunity, and those who are great are the ones who have recognized life as the opportunity for all things. Arts, sciences, and religions are monuments standing for what humanity has already accomplished. They stand as memorials to the unfolding mind of man, and through their avenues man passes to more efficient and more intelligent methods of attaining prescribed results. Blessed are those who can profit by the experiences of others, and can add to that which has already been built, their inspiration made real, their dream made practical. Those who give man the things he needs are seldom appreciated in their own age, but are later recognized as the saviors of the human race.

Masonry is a structure built of experience. Each stone is a sequential step in the unfolding of intelligence. The shrines of Masonry are ornamented by the jewels of a thousand ages; its rituals ring with the words of enlightened seers and illuminated sages. A hundred religions have brought their gifts of wisdom to its altar. Arts and sciences unnumbered have contributed to its symbolism. It is more than a faith: it is a path of certainty. It is more than a belief: it is a fact. Masonry is a university, teaching the liberal arts and sciences of the soul to all who will attend to its words. It is a shadow of the great Atlantean Mystery School, which stood with all its splendor in the ancient city of the Golden Gates, where now the turbulent Atlantic rolls in unbroken splendor. Its chairs are seats of learning; its pillars uphold an arch of universal education, not only in material things, but also in those qualities which are of the spirit. Upon its trestleboards are inscribed the sacred truths of all peoples and of all nations, and to those who understand its sacred depths has dawned the great reality. Masonry is, in truth, that long-lost thing which all peoples have sought in all ages. Masonry is the common denominator and the common divisor of human aspiration.

Most of the religions of the world are processions: one leads, and many follow. In the footsteps of the demigods, man follows in his search for truth and illumination. The Christian follows the gentle Nazarene up the winding slopes of Calvary. The Buddhist follows his great emancipator through his wanderings in the wilderness. The Mohammedan makes his pilgrimage across the desert sands to the black tent at Mecca. Truth leads, and ignorance follows in his train. Spirit blazes the trail, and matter follows behind. In the world today ideals live but a moment in their purity, before the gathering hosts of darkness snuff out the gleaming spark. The Mystery School, however, remains unmoved. It does not bring its light to man: man must bring his light to it. Ideals, coming into the world, become idols within a few short hours, but man, entering the gates of sanctuary, changes the idol back to an ideal.

Man is climbing an endless flight of steps, with

INTRODUCTION

his eyes turned toward the goal at the top. Many cannot see the goal, and only one or two steps are visible before them. He has learned, however, one great lesson, and that is, that as he builds his own character he is given strength to climb the steps. Hence a Mason is a builder of the temple of character. He is the architect of a sublime mystery— the gleaming, glowing temple of his own soul. He realizes that he best serves God when he joins with the Great Architect in building more noble structures in the universe below. All who are attempting to attain mastery through constructive efforts are Masons at heart, regardless of sects or religious beliefs. A Mason is not necessarily a member of a lodge. He is any person who tries every day to live the Masonic life, and to serve intelligently the needs of the Great Architect. The Masonic brother pledges himself to assist all other temple-builders in whatever extremity life may unfold, and in so doing he pledges himself to every stick and stone, to beast, God, and man, for they are all temple-builders, building more noble shrines wherein to worship the universal God.

The Masonic Lodge is a mystery school, a place where candidates are taken out of the follies and foibles of the world and are instructed in the mysteries of life, relationships, and the identity of that germ of spiritual essence in them, which is, in truth, the son of God, beloved of his Father. The Mason views life seriously, realizing that every wasted moment is a lost opportunity, and that Omnipotence is gained only through earnestness and endeavor. Above all other relationships he recognizes the universal brotherhood of living things. The clasped hands of his Lodge reflect his attitude toward all the world, for he is the comrade of all created things. He realizes also that his spirit is a glowing, gleaming jewel which he must enshrine within a holy temple built by the labor of his hands, the meditations of his heart, and the aspiration of his soul.

Masonry is a religion which is essentially creedless. It is the truer for it. Its brothers bow to truth regardless of the bearer; they serve light, instead of wrangling over the one who brings it. In this way they prove that they are seeking to know better the will and the dictates of the Invincible One. No truer religion exists in all the world than that all creatures gather together in comradeship and brotherhood, for the purpose of glorifying one God, and of building for Him a temple of constructive attitude and noble character.

II.

THE average Mason, as well as the modern student of Masonic ideals, little realizes or understands the cosmic obligation which he takes upon himself when he begins his search for the sacred truths of nature as they are concealed in the ancient and modern rituals. He must not lightly consider his vows, and if he would not bring upon himself years and ages of suffering he must cease to consider Masonry as merely a social or fraternal order. He must realize that the mystic teachings as perpetuated in the modern rites are sacred, and that powers unseen and unrecognized mold the destiny of those who consciously and of their own free will take upon themselves the obligations of the craft.

Masonry is not a material thing: it is a science of the soul; it is not a creed or doctrine but a universal expression of the Divine Wisdom.* The coming together of English guilds or even the

*This term is used as synonymous with a very secret and sacred philosophy that has existed for all time,. and has been the inspiration of the great saints and sages of all ages, i. e., the perfect wisdom of God, revealing itself through a secret hierarchy of the illumined minds.

23

building of Solomon's temple, as it is understood today, has little if anything to do with the true origin of Masonry, for Masonry does not deal with personalities. It is neither historical nor archaeological, but is a divine symbolic language perpetuating under certain concrete symbols the divine mysteries of the ancients. Only those who see in it a cosmic study, a life work, a spiritual inspiration to better thinking, better living, and better acting, with the spiritual attainment of enlightenment as the end, and with the daily life of the true Mason as the means, have gained even the slightest insight into the true mysteries of the ancient and accepted rite.

The age of the Masonic school is not to be calculated by hundreds or even thousands of years, for it never had any origin in the worlds of form. The world as we see it is merely an experimental laboratory in which man is laboring to build and express greater and more perfect vehicles. Into this laboratory pour thousands and millions of rays descending from the cosmic hierarchies.* These mighty globes and orbs which focus their energies upon mankind and mold his destiny do so in an orderly manner, each in its own way and place,

*The groups of celestial intelligencies governing the creative processes in cosmos.

and it is the working of these mystic hierarchies in the universe which forms the pattern around which the Masonic school has been built, for the true lodge of the Mason is the universe. Creedless and religionless he stands, a master of all faiths, and those who take up the study of Masonry without realizing the depth, the beauty, and the spiritual power of the thing they are analyzing can never gain anything of permanence from their studies. The age of the mystery schools can be traced by the true student back to the dawn of time, hundreds of millions, yes, billions of years ago, when the temple of the Solar Man was in the making. That was the first Temple of the King, and there in the dawn of time were given and laid down the true mysteries of the ancient lodge, and · it was the gods of creation and the spirits of the dawn who first tiled the Master's lodge.

The initiated brother realizes that his so-called symbols and rituals are merely blinds built by the wise to perpetuate ideas incomprehensible to the average individual. He also realizes that few Masons of today know or appreciate the mystic meaning concealed within these rituals. With religious faith we perpetuate the form, worshiping it instead of the life, but those who have not gathered the truth from the crystallized ritual, those who have not liberated the spiritual germ from the shell of empty words, are not Masons, regardless of their physical degrees.

In the work we are taking up it is not the intention to dwell upon the modern concepts of the craft but to consider Masonry as it really is to those who know, a great cosmic organism whose true brothers and children are tied together not by spoken oaths but by lives so lived that they are capable of seeing through the blank wall and opening the window which is now concealed by the rubbish of materiality. When this is done and the mysteries of the universe unfold before the aspiring candidate, then in truth he discovers what Masonry really is; its material aspects interest him no longer for he has unmasked the mystery school which he is capable of recognizing only when he himself has spiritually become a member of it.

There is no doubt in the minds of those who have examined and studied its ancient lore that Masonry, like the universe itself, which is the greatest of all schools, deals with the unfolding of a threefold principle, for all the universe is governed by the same three kings who are called the builders of the Masonic temple. They are not personalities but principles, great intelligent energies and powers which in God, man, and the universe have charge of the molding of cosmic substance into the habitation of the living king, the temple built through millions of years of first unconscious and then conscious effort on the part of every individual who is expressing in his daily life the creative principles of the three kings.

The true brother of the ancient craft realized that the completion of the temple he was building to the King of the universe was a duty or rather a privilege which he owed to his God, to his brother, and to himself. He knew that certain steps must be taken and that his temple must be built according to plan, but today it seems that the plan is lost, for in the majority of cases Masonry is no longer operative but is merely a speculative idea and must remain so until each brother, reading the mystery of his symbols and pondering over the beautiful allegories unfolded in his ritual, realizes that he himself contains the keys and the plans so long lost to his craft and that if he would ever learn Masonry he must unlock its doors with the key filed from the base metals of his own being.

True Masonry is esoteric; it is not a thing of this world; all that we have here is a link, a doorway, through which the student may pass into the unknown. It has nothing to do with things of form save that it realizes that form is molded by and manifests the life it contains, and the student is seeking to so mold his life that the form will glorify the God within whose temple he is slowly building as he awakens one after another the work-men within himself and sets them to the carrying out of the plan which has been given him out of heaven.

So far as it is possible to discover, ancient Masonry and the beautiful cosmic allegories that it teaches, perpetuated through hundreds of lodges and ancient mysteries, forms the oldest of the mystery schools;* and its preservation through the ages has not depended upon itself as an exoteric body of partly evolved individuals but upon a concealed brotherhood, the esoteric side of Masonry. All of the great mystery schools have hierarchies upon the spiritual planes of nature which are expressing themselves in this world through creeds and organisms. The true student is seeking to lift himself from the exoteric body upward spiritually until he joins the esoteric group which, without a lodge on the physical plane of nature, is still greater by far than all the lodges of which it is the central fire. These spiritual instructors of humanity are forced to labor in the concrete world with things comprehensible to the concrete mind, and there

*This is a term used by the ancients to designate the esoteric side of their religious ceremonials. The candidate passing through these mysteries was initiated into the mysteries of Nature and the hidden side of natural law.

comes through to man the meaning of the allegories and symbols which surround his exoteric work as soon as he prepares himself to receive them. The true Mason realizes that the work of the mystery schools in the world is of an inclusive rather than an exclusive nature, and that the only lodge which is broad enough to express his ideals is the one whose dome is the heavens, whose pillars are the corners of creation, whose checkerboard floor is composed of the crossing currents of human emotion, and whose altar is the human heart. Creeds cannot bind the true seeker for truth. The Mason, realizing the unity of all truth, also realizes that the hierarchies laboring with him have given him in his varying degrees the mystic, spiritual rituals of all the mystery schools in the world, and if he would fill his place in the plan he must not enter this sacred study for what he can get out of it but that he may learn how better to put more in.

Masonry has concealed within it the mystery of creation, the answer to the problem of existence, and the path which the student must walk in order to join those who are really the living powers behind the thrones of modern national and international affairs. The true student realizes most of all that the taking of degrees does not make a man a Mason; a Mason is not appointed, he is evolved, and he must realize that the position he holds in the exoteric lodge means nothing compared to his position in the spiritual lodge of life. He must forever cast out of his being the idea that he can be told or instructed in the sacred mysteries or that his being a member of an organization improves him in any way; he must realize that his duty is to build and evolve the sacred teaching in his own being: that nothing but his own purified being can unlock the door to the sealed libraries of human consciousness, and that his Masonic rites must eternally be speculative until he makes them operative by living the life of the mystic Mason. His karmic responsibilities increase with his opportunities. Those who are surrounded with knowledge and opportunity for self-improvement and make nothing of these opportunities are the lazy workmen who will be spiritually if not physically cast out of the temple of the king.

The Masonic order is not a social organization, but truly is composed of those who have banded themselves together to learn and to apply the principles of mysticism and the occult rites. They are or should be philosophers, sages, and soberminded individuals who have dedicated themselves upon the living altar of the gods and who have vowed by all that they hold dear that the world shall be better, wiser, and happier because they have lived. Those who enter these mystic rites and pass between the pillars seeking either prestige or commercial advantage are blasphemers, and while in this world we may count them as successful they are the cosmic failures who have barred themselves out from the true rite whose keynote is unselfishness and whose workers have renounced the things of earth.

In ancient times many years of preparation were required before the neophyte was permitted to enter the temple of the mysteries. In this way those who were shallow, the curiosity seekers, the faint of heart, and those unable to withstand the temptations of life were not chosen, but automatically withdrew themselves from a price which was greater than they would pay, and he who did pass between the pillars entered the temple realizing his sublime opportunity, his divine obligation, and the mystic privilege which he had earned for himself through years of special preparation. Only those are truly Masons who enter their temple in reverence, who are seeking not the passing things of life but the treasures which are eternal, whose one desire in life is to know the true mystery of the craft that they may join as honest workmen those who have gone before as builders of the universal temple. The Masonic ritual is not a ceremony, but a life to be lived. Those who are really Masons are those who have dedicated their lives and their souls on the altar of the living flame and who are glad to labor in any way in the construction of the one universal building of which they are the workmen and their God the living Architect. When we have Masons like this the craft will again be operative, the flaming triangle will shine forth with the greater lustre, the dead builder will rise from his tomb, and the lost Word so long concealed from the profane will blaze forth again with the power that makes all things new.

In the pages that follow there has been set down a number of thoughts for the study and consideration of temple builders, craftsmen and artisan alike. They are the keys which if read will leave the student still in ignorance but if lived will change the speculative Masonry of today into the operative Masonry of tomorrow, when each builder, realizing his own place, will see things which he never saw before, not because they were not there but because he was blind. And there are none so blind as those who will not see.

The Emerald Tablet of Hermes

This ancient tablet was the first revelation of God to man. While its mystery is practically unknown to this age it undoubtedly was the basis of the Masonic Legend of Hiram. -:- -:- -:-

THE EMERALD TABLET
OF HERMES
(TABULA SMARAGDINA)

The Emerald Tablet, the Most Ancient Monument of the Chaldeans Concerning the Lapis Philosophoram.

THE Emerald Tablet of Hermes, illustrated on the opposite page, introduces us to King Hiram, the hero of the Masonic legend. The name *Hiram* is taken from the Chaldee *Chiram*. The first two large words mean *THE SECRET WORK*. The second line in large letters—*CHIRAM TELAT MECHASOT*—means *Chiram, the universal agent, one in essence, but three in aspect*. Translated the body of the tablet reads as follows:

"It is true and no lie, certain and to be depended upon, that the superior agrees with the inferior, and the inferior with the superior, to effect that one truly wonderful work. As all things owe their existence to the will of the *Only One*, so all things owe their origin to *Only One Thing*, the most hidden, by the arrangement of the *Only God*. The father of that *Only One Thing* is the *Sun*; its mother is the *Moon*; the wind carries it in its wings; but its nurse is a *Spiritual Earth*. That

33

Only One Thing is the father of all things in the universe. Its power is perfect after it has been united to a spiritual earth. Separate that spiritual earth from the dense or crude earth by means of a gentle heat, with much attention. In great measure it ascends from earth up into heaven; and descends again, new-born, on the earth, and the superior and the inferior are increased in power. By this thou wilt partake of the honors of the whole earth and darkness shall fly from thee. This is the strength of all powers; with this thou wilt be able to overcome all things and to transmute *all that is fine* and all that is *coarse.* In this manner the world was created, but the arrangements that follow this road are hidden. For this reason I am called *CHIRAM TELAT MECHASOT, one in essence,* but *three in aspect. In this trinity* is hidden the wisdom of the whole world. It is ended now what I have said concerning the effect *of the sun.*

FINIS OF THE TABULA SMARAGDINA"

In a rare, unpublished old manuscript dealing with early Masonic and Hermetic mysteries, we find the following information concerning the mysterious universal agent referred to as "Chiram" (Hiram):

THE EMERALD TABLET OF HERMES

The sense of this emerald tablet can sufficiently convince us that the author was well acquainted with the secret operations of nature and with the secret work of the philosophers (alchemists and Hermetic philosophists). He likewise well knew and believed in the true God.

It has been believed since several ages that Cham, one of the sons of Noah, is the author of this monument of antiquity. A very ancient author, whose name is not known, who lived several centuries before Christ, mentions this tablet, and says that he had seen it in Egypt, at the court; that it was a precious stone, an emerald, whereon these characters were represented in bas relief, not engraved.

He states that it was in his time esteemed over two thousand years old, and that the matter of this emerald had once been in a fluid state like melted glass, and had been cast in a mold, and that to this flux the artist had given the hardness of a natural and genuine emerald, by art. (Alchemical art.)

The Cananites were called the Phoenicians by the Greeks, who have told us that they had Hermes for one of their kings. There is a great relation between Chiram and Hermes.

Chiram is a word composed out of three words, denoting the universal spirit, the essence whereof the whole creation does consist, and the object of Chaldean Egyptian and genuine natural philosophy, according to its inward principles or properties. The three Hebrew words *Chama, Rauch,* and *Majim*, mean respectively *Fire*, *Air*, and *Water*, while their initial consonants, *Ch*, *R*, *M*, give us *Chiram*, that invisible essence which is the father of earth, fire, air and water, because, although immaterial in its own invisible nature, as the unmoved and electrical fire, when moved it becomes light and visible; and when collected and agitated, becomes heat and visible and tangible fire; and when it associates with humidity it becomes material. The word *Chiram* has been metamorphosed into *Hermes* and also into *Herman*, and the translators of the Bible have made *Chiram* by changing *Chet* into *He;* both of these Hebrew word signs being very similar.

In the old word *Hermaphrodite*, a word invented by the philosophers, we find *Hermes* changed to *Herm*, signifying *Chiram*, or the universal agent, and *Aphrodite*, the passive principle of humidity, who is also called *Venus*, and is said to have been produced and generated by the sea.

We also read that Hiram (*Chiram*), or the universal agent, assisted King Solomon to build the temple; no doubt as Solomon possessed wisdom, he understood what to do with the corporealized universal agent. The Talmud of the Jews says that King Solomon built the temple by the assistance of Schamir. Now this word signifies the sun, as the large machine which is perpetually collecting the Omnipresent, surrounding, electrical fire, or Spiritus Mundi, and sends it constantly to us in the planets, in a visible manner called *light*.

This electrical flame, corporealized and regen-

36

erated into the stone of the philosophers, enabled King Solomon to produce the immense quantities of gold and silver used to build and decorate his temple.

These ancient paragraphs from an ancient philosopher may assist the Masonic student of to-day to realize the tremendous and undreamed-of store of knowledge that lies behind the allegory, which he often hears but seldom analyzes. Hiram, the universal agent, might be translated *Vita*, the power eternally building and unfolding the bodies of man. The use and abuse of energy is the key to the Masonic legend; in fact, it is the key to all things in nature. And Hiram, as the triple energy, one in source but three in aspect, can almost be called ether, the unknown hypothetical element, which carries the impulses of the gods through the macrocosmic nervous system of the Infinite. Hermes, or Mercury, was the messenger of the gods, and ether carries impulse upon its wings. The solving of the mystery of ether, or, if you prefer to call it such, vibrant space, is the great problem of Masonry. This ether, as a hypothetical medium, brings energy to the three bodies of thought, emotion, and action, and in this way Chiram, the one in essence, becomes three in aspect—mental, emotional, and vital. The work which follows is an

effort to bring to light other forgotten and neg-
lected elements of the Masonic rites, and to em-
phasize the spirit of Hiram as the universal agent.

Masonry is essentially mysterious, ritualistic,
and ceremonial; but these things represent, in concrete form, only abstract truth. And earth (or
substance) smothering energy (or vitality) is the
mystery behind the murder of the builder.

Text

Remember now thy creator in the days of thy youth, while the evil days come not, nor the years draw nigh, when thou shalt say, I have no pleasure in them; while the sun, or the moon, or the stars be not darkened, nor the clouds return after the rain; in the day when the keepers of the house shall tremble, and the strong men shall bow themselves, and the grinders cease, because they are few; and those that look out of the windows be darkened, and the door shall be shut in the streets; when the sound of the grinding is low, and he shall rise up at the voice of the bird, and all the daughters of music shall be brought low. Also when they shall be afraid of that which is high and fear shall be in the way, and the almond-tree shall flourish, and the grasshoppers shall be a burden, and desire shall fail; because man goeth to his long home, and the mourners go about the streets: or ever the silver cord be loosed, or the golden bowl be broken at the fountain, or the wheel at the cistern. Then shall the dust return to the earth as it was; and the spirit shall return unto God Who gave it.—*Ecclesiastes*, 12:1—7.

39

TEMPLE BUILDERS

You are the temple builders of the future. With your hands must be raised the domes and spires of a coming civilization. Upon the foundation you have laid, tomorrow shall build a far more noble edifice. Builders of the temple of character wherein should dwell an enlightened spirit, truer of the rock of relationship, molder of those vessels created to contain the oil of life, up, and to the tasks appointed! Never before in the history of men have you had the opportunity that now confronts you. The world waits—waits for the illuminated one who shall come from between the pillars of the portico. Hoodwinked and bound humanity seeks entrance to the temple of wisdom. Fling wide the gate, and let the worthy enter. Fling wide the gate, and let the light shine forth, for that light is the life of men. Hasten to complete the dwelling of the Lord. The Spirit of God may come and dwell among his people, sanctified and ordained according to his law.

IN THE FIELDS OF CHAOS

THE first flush of awakening life thrilled and gleamed through the darkness of cosmic night, turned the darkness of negation into the dim twilight of unfolding being, and cast its faint glimmering rays over a strange form which stood alone on the cloudy banks of swirling substances. Robed in shimmery blue vapor of mystery, his head encircled by a golden crown of flaming light, a mystic stranger stood there, his form divine shrouded in the folds of chaos whose darkness fled before the rays that poured like streams of living fire from his gigantic, misty form silhouetted in faint relief against the shadowed gateways of eternity.

From some cosmos greater far than ours this mystic visitor came, answering the call of Divinity. From star to star he strode and from world to universe He was known and yet concealed forever by the filmy garments of chaotic night. Suddenly the clouds broke and a wondrous light descended from somewhere among the seething waves of force; it bathed this lonely form in a radiance celestial, each sparkling crystal of mist gleaming like a diamond bathed in the living fire of the Divine.

Two great forms appeared in the gleaming flame of cosmic light bordered by the dark clouds of not-being and a mighty Voice thrilled through eternity, each sparkling atom dancing, swaying and swirling with the power of The Creator's Word* while the great, blue-robed figure bowed in awe before the footstool of His Maker and a great hand reached down from heaven, its fingers extended in benediction.

"Of all creation I have chosen you and upon you my seal is placed; you are the chosen instrument of my hand and I choose you to be. the builder of my Temple; you shall raise its pillars and tile its floor; you shall ornament it with metals and with jewels and you shall be the master of my workmen; into your hands I place the plans and here on the tracing board of living substance I impress the plan you are to follow, tracing its every letter and angle in the fiery lines of my moving finger. Hiram Abiff, chosen builder of your Father's house, up and to your work; yonder are the fleecy clouds, the gray mist of dawn, the gleams of heavenly light, and the darkness of the

*The creative fiat, or rate of vibration through which all things are created.

sleep of creation. From these shall you build, without the sound of hammers or the voice of workmen, the temple of your God, eternal in the heavens. The swirling, ceaseless motion of negation you shall chain to grind your stones. Among these spirits of not-being shall you slack your lime and lay your footings, for I have watched you through the years of your youth; I have guided you through the days of your manhood. I have weighed you in the balance and you have not been found wanting. Therefore, to you give I the glory of work, and here ordain you as the Builder of my House. Unto you I give the word of the Master Builder; unto you I give the tools of the craft; unto you I give the power that has been vested in me: be faithful unto these things; bring them back when you have finished, and I will give you the name known to God alone. So mote it be."

The great light died out of the heavens, the streaming fingers of living light vanished through the misty, lonely twilight, and again covered not-being with its sable mantle. Hiram again stood alone, gazing out into the endless ocean of oblivion: nothing but swirling, seething matter as far as eye could see. Then, rising, he straightened his shoulders and taking the trestle board in his hands and clasping to his heart the Word of the Master which sparkled and gleamed in the darkness of the night, Hiram Abiff slowly walked out over the clouds and vanished through the mist which swallowed up even the glowing spark of the Master's Word.

How may man measure timeless eternity? Ages passed, and the lonely builder labored with his plan with only love and humility in his heart, his hand molding the darkness which he blessed while his eyes were raised above where the Great Light had shone down from heaven. In the divine solitude he labored, no voice to cheer, no spirit to condemn; alone in the boundless all with the great chill of the morning mist upon his brow, but his heart still warm with the light of the Master's Word. It seemed a hopeless battle: no single pair of hands could mold that darkness; no single heart, no matter how true, could be great enough to send the pulsing cosmic love into the cold mist of oblivion. The darkness settled ever closer about him, the misty fingers of negation twined around his being, and still with divine trust the builder labored; with divine hope he laid his footings, and from the boundless clay he made the molds to cast his sacred ornaments. Slowly the building grew and dim forms molded by the Master's hand took shape about him. Three great, soulless creatures had the Master fashioned, great, towering beings which appeared in half darkness like grim spectres.

They were three builders he had blessed and now in stately file they passed before him, and Hiram held out his arms to his creation, saying, "Brothers, I have built you for your works, I have formed you to labor with me in the building of the Master's house; you are the children of my being; I have labored with you, now labor with me for the glory of our God."

But the spectres laughed and turned upon their maker, and striking him with his own tools given to him by God out of heaven, they left their Grand Master dying in the midst of his labors, broken and crushed by the threefold powers of cosmic night. As he lay bleeding at the feet of his handiwork the martyr builder raised his eyes to the seething clouds, and his face was sweet with divine love and cosmic understanding as he prayed unto the Master who had sent him forth.

"O Master of Workmen, Great Architect of the universe, my labors are not finished. Why must they always remain undone? I have not completed the thing for which Thou hast sent me into being, for my very creations have turned against me and the tools Thou gavest me have destroyed me. The children that I formed in love, in ignorance have murdered me. Here, Father, is the Word Thou gavest me now red with my own blood. O, Master, I return it to Thee for I have kept it sacred in my heart. Here are the tools, the tracing board, and the vessels I have wrought. Around me stand the ruins of my temple which I must leave. Unto Thee, O God, the divine Knower of all things, I return them all, realizing that in Thy good time lies the fulfillment of all things. Thou, O God, knowest our downsitting and our uprising and Thou understandeth our thoughts afar off. In Thy name, Father, I have labored and in Thy cause I die, a faithful builder."

The Master fell back, his upturned face sweet in the last repose of death, and the light rays no longer pouring from him. The gray clouds gathered closer as though to form a winding sheet around the body of their murdered Master.

Suddenly the heavens opened again and a great glow descended as a sparkling ray and, surrounding the form of Hiram, bathed it in a light celestial, and again the Voice spoke from the heavens above where the Great King sat above the clouds of creation, "He is not dead: he is asleep. Who shall awaken him? His labors are not done, and in death he guards the sacred relics more closely than ever, for the Word and the tracing board are his—I have given them to him. But he must remain asleep until these three who have slain him shall bring him back to life, for every wrong must be righted, and the slayers of my house, the destroyers of my temple, must labor in the place of their builder until they raise their Master from the dead."

The three murderers fell on their knees and raised their hands to heaven as though to ward off the light which unearthed their crime: "O God, great is our sin, for we have slain our Grand Master, Hiram Abiff! Just is Thy punishment and as we have slain him we now dedicate our lives to his resurrection. The first was our human weakness, the second our sacred duty."

"Be it so," answered the Voice from Heaven. The great Light vanished and the clouds of darkness and mist concealed the body of the murdered Master. It was swallowed up in the darkness which, swirling and swaying, left no mark, no gravestone, on the place where the builder had lain.

"O God!" cried the three murderers, "where shall we find our Master now?"

The hand reached down again from the Great Unseen and a tiny lamp was handed them whose oil flame burned silently and clearly in the darkness. "By this light which I have given ye shall ye seek him whom ye have slain."

The three forms surrounded the light and bowed in prayer and thanksgiving for this solitary gleam which was to light the darkness of their way. From somewhere above in the regions of not-being the great Voice spoke, a thundering Voice that filled Chaos with its sound: "He cometh forth as a flower and is cut down; he fleeth also as a shadow and continueth not; as the waters fail from the sea and the flood decayeth and drieth up, so man lieth down and riseth not again. Yet I have compassion upon the children of my creation; I administer unto them in time of trouble and save them with an everlasting salvation. Seek ye where the broken twig lies and where the dead stick molds away, where the clouds float together and where the stones rest by the hillside, for all these mark the grave of Hiram who has carried my Will with him to the tomb. This eternal quest is yours until ye have found your Builder, until the cup giveth up its secret, until the grave giveth up its ghosts. I shall speak to ye no more until ye have found and raised my beloved Son, and have listened to the words of my Messenger and with Him as your guide have finished the temple which I shall then inhabit. Amen."

The gray dawn still lay asleep in the arms of darkness. Out through the great mystery of not-being all was silence, unknowable. Through the misty dawn, like strange phantoms of a dream, three figures wandered over the great Unknown carrying in their hands a tiny light, the lamp given

to them by their Builder's Father. They wandered
eternally in search of a silent grave: over stick and
stone and cloud and star they wandered, stopping
again and again to explore the depths of some
mystic recess, praying for liberation from their
endless search, yet bound by vows eternal to raise
the Builder they had slain, whose grave was marked
by the broken twig, and whose body was laid away
in the white winding sheet of death somewhere
over the brow of the eternal hill.

MOTIVE

What motive leads the Masonic candidate out of
the world and up the winding stairway to the light?
He alone can truly know, for in his heart is hidden
the motive of his works. Is he seeking the light of
the East? Is he seeking wisdom eternal? Does
he bring his life and offer it upon the altar of the
Most High? Of all things, motive is most important. Though we fail again and again, if our motive
be true, we are victorious. Though time after time
we succeed, if our motive be unworthy, we have
failed. Enter the temple in reverence, for it is in
truth the dwelling place of a Great Spirit, the Spirit
of Masonry. Masonry is an ordainer of kings. Its
hand has moved the destinies of worlds, and the perfect fruitage of its molding is an honest man. What
nobler thing can be accomplished than the illumination of ignorance? What greater task is there
than the joyous labor of service? And what nobler
man can there be than that Mason who serves his
Lights, and is himself a light unto his fellowmen?

Chapter One

THE CANDIDATE

THERE comes a time in the individual growth of every living thing when it realizes with dawning consciousness that it is a prisoner. While apparently free to move and have its being, the struggling life cognizes through ever greater vehicles its own limitation. It is at this point that man cries out with ever greater power to be liberated from the binding ties which, though invisible to mortal eyes, still chain him with bonds far more terrible than those of a physical prison.

Many have read the story of the prisoner of Shiloah who as the years rolled by paced back and forth in the narrow confines of his prison cell, while the blue waters rolled ceaselessly above his head and the only sound that broke the stillness of his eternal night was the constant swishing and lapping of the waves. We pity the prisoner in his physical tomb and as we see stone walls surrounding man we are sad at heart for we know how life loves liberty. But there is one prisoner whose plight is far worse than that of those of earth. He has not even the narrow confines of a prison cell around Him; He cannot pace to and fro to wear into ruts by His ceaseless striding the cobblestones of a dungeon floor. That eternal Prisoner is Life, prisoned within the dark stone walls of matter with not a single ray to brighten the blackness of His fate; he fights eternally for life, praying in the dark confines of gloomy walls for light and opportunity. This is the eternal Prisoner who through the ceaseless ages of cosmic unfoldment, through forms unnumbered and species now unknown, strives eternally to liberate Himself and to gain self-conscious expression, the birthright of every created thing. He awaits the day when standing upon the rocks that now form His shapeless tomb, He may raise His arms to heaven, bathed in the sunlight of spiritual freedom, free to join the sparkling atoms and dancing light-beings released from the bonds of prison wall and tomb.

Around Life—that wondrous germ in the heart of every living thing, that sacred Prisoner in His gloomy cell, that Master Builder laid away in the grave of matter—has been built the wondrous legend of the Holy Sepulchre. The mystic philosophers of the ages, under allegories unnumbered, have perpetuated this wonderful story, and among the Craft Masons it forms the mystic ritual of Hiram, the Master Builder, murdered in his temple by the very builders who should have served him as he labored to perfect the dwelling place of his God.

Matter is the tomb: it is the dead wall of substances whose lives have not as yet been awakened into the pulsating energies of Spirit. It exists in many degrees and forms, not only in the chemical elements which form the solids of our universe, but in finer and more subtle substances. These, though expressing through emotion and thought, are still beings of the world of form. These substances form the great cross of matter which opposes the growth of all things and by opposition makes all growth possible. It is the great cross of hydrogen, nitrogen, oxygen, and carbon upon which even the life germ in protoplasm is crucified and suspended in agony. These substances are incapable of giving it adequate expression. The Spirit within cries out for freedom: freedom to be, to express, to manifest its true place in the Great Plan of cosmic unfoldment.

It is this great yearning within the heart of man which sends him slowly onward toward the gate of the Temple; it is this inner urge for greater understanding and greater light which brought into being through the law of necessity the great cosmic Masonic Lodge dedicated to those lives which were seeking union with the Powers of Light that their prison walls might be removed. This shell cannot be discarded: it must be raised into union with the Life; each dead, crystallized atom in the human body must be set vibrating and spinning to a higher rate of consciousness. Through purification, through knowledge, and through service to his fellow-man the candidate sequentially unfolds these mystic properties, building better and more perfect bodies through which his higher life secures ever greater manifestation. The expression of man through constructive thought, emotion, and action liberates the higher nature from bodies which in their crystallized states are incapable of giving him his natural opportunities.

In Masonry this crystallized substance of matter is called the grave and the Holy Sepulchre. It is within this grave that the lost Builder lies and with Him are the plans of the temple and the Master's Word, and it is this Builder, our Grand Master, that we must seek and, finding, raise from the dead and restore to Him the crown of Spirit so long missing from the temple of our King. This noble Son of Light cries out to us in every expression of matter. Every stick and stone marks His resting place, and the sprig of acacia promises that through the long winter of spiritual darkness, when the sun does not shine for man, this Light still is—still waits for the day of liberation when each one of us shall raise Him by the grip of the Grand Master, the true grip of a Master Mason. We cannot hear this Voice that calls eternally, but we feel that inner urge, a great unknown something pulls at our heartstrings, and as the ages roll by, the deep desire to be greater, to live better, and to think God's thoughts builds within ourselves the qualifications of a candidate who, when truly asked why he takes the path, would answer if he knew mentally the things he feels, "I hear a voice that cries out to me from flora and fauna, from stones, from clouds, from the very heaven itself. Each fiery atom spinning and twisting in cosmos cries out to me with the voice of my Master. I can hear Hiram Abiff, my Grand Master, calling, crying out with agony, the agony of life hidden within the darkness of its prison walls, seeking for the expression which I have denied it, striving, laboring, to bring closer the day of its liberation, and I have learned to know that I am responsible for those walls. My daily actions are the things which as ruffians and traitors are murdering my God."

There are many legends of the Holy Sepulchre which has for so many ages been in the hands of the infidel and which the Christian worlds sought to retake in the days of the Crusades. Few Masons realize that this Holy Sepulchre, this tomb, is in reality negation, crystallization, matter that has sealed within itself the Spirit of Life which must remain in darkness until the growth of each individual being gives it walls of glowing gold and changes its stones into windows. As we develop better and better vehicles of expression these walls slowly expand until at last Spirit rises triumphant from its tomb and, blessing the very walls that confined it, raises them to union with itself.

We may first consider the murderers of Hiram. These three ruffians, who, when the Builder seeks to leave his temple, strike him with the tools of his own craft until finally they slay him and bring the temple down in destruction upon their own heads, symbolize the three expressions of our own lower natures which are in truth the murderers of the good within ourselves which they pervert as soon as we seek to manifest it. These three may be called thought, desire, and action. When purified and transmuted they are three glorious avenues through which may manifest the great life power of the three kings, the glowing builders of the cosmic lodge which manifest in this world as spiritual thought, constructive emotion, and useful daily labor in the various places and positions where we find ourselves while carrying on the Master's work. These three form the Flaming Triangle which glorifies every living Mason, but when crystallized and perverted they form a triangular

prison through which the light cannot shine and
the Life is forced to pace back and forth in the
dim darkness of despair, until man himself through
his higher understanding shall liberate the energies and powers which are indeed the builders and
glorifiers of his Father's House.

Now let us consider how these three fiery kings
of the dawn became, through perversion of their
manifestation by man, the ruffians who murdered
Hiram, who represents the energizing powers of
cosmos which course through the blood of every
living being, seeking to beautify and perfect the
temple it would build according to the plan laid
down on the tracing board by the Master Architect
of the universe. First in the mind is one of the
three kings, or rather we shall say a pole through
which he manifests, for King Solomon is the power
of mind which when perverted becomes a destroyer
who tears down with the very powers which nour-
ish and build. The right application of thought,
when seeking the answer to the cosmic problem of
destiny, liberates man's spirit which soars above
the concrete through that wonderful power of mind,
with its dreams and its ideals.

When man's thoughts rise upward, when he
pushes backward the darkness with reason and
logic, then indeed the builder is liberated from his
dungeon and the light pours in, bathing him with

life and power. This light enables us to seek more clearly the mystery of creation and to find with greater certainty our place in the great plan, for as man unfolds his bodies he gains talents with which he can explore the mysteries of nature and search for the hidden workings of the Divine. Through these powers the Builder is liberated and his consciousness goes forth conquering and to conquer. These higher ideals, these spiritual concepts, these altruistic, philanthropic, educative applications of thought power glorify the Builder, for they give the power of expression; and those who can express themselves are free. When man can mold his thoughts, his emotions, and his actions into faithful expressions of his highest ideals then liberty is his, *for ignorance is the darkness of chaos and knowledge is the light of cosmos.*

In spite of the fact that many of us live apparently to gratify the desires of the body and as servants of the lower nature, still there is within each of us a power which may remain latent for a great length of time. This power lives eternities perhaps, and yet at some time during our growth there comes a great desire, a yearning for freedom, when, having discovered that the pleasures of sense gratification are eternally elusive and unsatisfying, we make an examination of ourselves and begin to realize that there are greater reasons for our being. It is sometimes reason, sometimes suffering, sometimes a great desire to be helpful, that brings out the first latent powers which show that one long wandering in the darkness is about to take the path that leads to Light. Having lived life in all its experiences he has learned to realize that all the manifestations of being, all the various experiences through which he passes, are steps leading in one direction and that consciously or unconsciously all souls are being led to the portico of the temple where for the first time they see and realize the glory of divinity. It is then that they understand the age-old allegory of the martyred Builder and feel his power within themselves crying out from the prison of materiality. Nothing else seems worth while; and regardless of cost, suffering, or the taunts of the world, the candidate slowly ascends the steps that lead to the temple eternal. The reason that governs cosmos he does not know, the laws which mold his being he does not realize, but he does know that somewhere behind the veil of human ignorance there is an eternal light toward which step by step he must labor. With his eyes fixed on the heavens above and his hands clasped in prayer he passes slowly as a candidate up the steps. In fear and trembling, yet with a divine realization of good, he taps on the door and awaits in silence the answer from within.

TRANSMUTATION

Masonry is eternal truth, personified, idealized, and yet made simple. Eternal truth alone can serve it. Virtue is its priest, patience its warden, illumination its master. The world cannot know this, however, save when Masons in their daily life prove that it is so. Its truth is divine, and is not to be desecrated or defamed by the thoughtlessness of its keepers. Its temple is a holy place, to be entered in reverence. Material thoughts and material dissensions must be left without its gate. They may not enter. Only the pure of heart, regenerated and transmuted, may pass the sanctity of its veil. The schemer has no place in its ranks, nor the materialist in its shrine, for Masons walk on hallowed ground, sanctified by the veneration of ages. Let the tongue be stilled, let the heart be stilled, let the mind be stilled. In reverence and in the silence, stillness shall speak: the voice of stillness is the voice of the Creator. Show your light and your power to men, but before God what have you to offer, save in humility? Your robes, your tinsel, and your jewels mean naught to Him, until your own body and soul, gleaming with the radiance of perfection, become the living ornaments of your Lodge.

Chapter Two

THE ENTERED APPRENTICE

THERE are three grand steps in the unfoldment of the human soul before it completes the dwelling place of the spirit. These have been called respectively youth, manhood, and old age; or, as the Mason would say, the Entered Apprentice, the Fellow Craft, and the Master Builder. All life passes through these three grand stages of human consciousness. They can be listed as the man on the outside looking in, the man going in, and the man inside. The path of human life is governed as all things are by the laws of analogy, and as at birth we start our pilgrimage through youth, manhood, and old age, so the spiritual consciousness of man in his cosmic path of unfoldment passes from unconsciousness to perfect consciousness in the grand Lodge of the universe. Before the initiation* of Entered Apprentice degree can be properly under-

---

*Initiation is the process spiritually of being instructed in the processes of causes of causation, which lie behind every effect of Nature.

stood and appreciated, certain requirements must be considered: not merely those of the physical world but also those of the spiritual world.

The Mason must realize that his true initiation is a spiritual and not a physical ritual, and that his initiation into the living temple of the spiritual hierarchy regulating Masonry may not occur until years after he has taken the physical degree, or spiritually he may be a Grand Master before he comes into the world. There are probably few examples in the entire history of Masonry where the spiritual ordination of the aspiring seeker took place at the same time as the physical initiation, because the true initiation depends upon the building of certain soul qualities—an individual and personal matter which is left entirely to the conscious effort of the mystic Mason and which he must carry out in silence and alone.

The court of the tabernacle of the ancient Jews was divided into three parts: the outer court, the holy place, and the most Holy of Holies. These three divisions represent the three grand divisions of human consciousness. The degree of Entered Apprentice is acquired when the student signifies his intention to take the rough ashler* which he cuts from the quarry and prepare it for the truing of

*A stone, or block of granite.

the Fellow Craft. In other words, the first degree is really one of preparations; it is a material step dealing with material things, for all spiritual life must be raised upon a material foundation.

Seven is the number of the Entered Apprentice as it relates to the seven liberal arts and sciences,* and these are the powers with which the Entered Apprentice must labor before he is worthy to go onward into the more elevated and advanced degrees. Those who believe that they can reach the spiritual planes of nature without first passing through and conquering, and by conquering, mold matter into expressions of spiritual power, are much mistaken, for the first stage in the growth of a Master Mason is the mastery of the concrete conditions of life and the developing, through exercise on this plane, of nature sense centers which will later become channels for the expression of spiritual truths.

All growth is a gradual procedure carried on in an orderly, masterly way as is shown by the opening and closing of a lodge. The universe is divided into groups and these groups are divided from each other by the rates of vibration which pass through them. As the spiritual consciousness is

---

*The seven liberal arts and sciences are: Astronomy, music, geometry, arithmetic, logic, rhetoric and grammar.

carried through the chain, those who are lower lose connection with it when it has raised itself above their level, until finally only the Grand Masters are capable of remaining in session, and unknown even to the Master Mason it passes back again to the spiritual hierarchy from which it came.

Action is the lost key of the Entered Apprentice lodge. All growth is the result of exercise and the heightening of vibratory rates. It is through exercise that the muscles of the human body are strengthened; it is through the seven liberal arts and sciences that the mind of man receives certain impulses which in turn start into action centers of consciousness within himself. These centers of consciousness will later through still greater development give fuller expression to these inner powers; but the Entered Apprentice has as his first duty the awakening of these powers, and, like the youth of whom he is a symbol, his ideals and mind and labors must be tied closely to concrete things. For him both points of the compass are under the square; for him the reasons which manifest through the heart and mind, the two polarities of expression, are darkened and concealed beneath the square which measures the block of bodies. He knows not the reason why, his work is to do and to follow the directions of those whose knowledge

The candidate at the gates of the Temple of Wisdom. Bound with the cable-tow of limitation, poor in spirit and in body, man seeks admittance to the University of Understanding. -:-

In the Ancient Mysteries the seven lower steps represented the seven liberal arts and sciences—the problems which first confront the seeker after higher light. Next above were the five steps of the senses and emotions, and highest of all were the three which were symbolic of the Trinity of God in man. In the Masonic lodges the order of the steps is reversed. -:-   -:-   -:-   -:-   -:-   -:-

is greater than his own; but as the result of his doing and the application of energies through action and reaction, he slowly builds and evolves the powers of discrimination and the strength of character which mark the Fellow Craft degree.

Of course the rough ashler symbolizes the body. It also represents cosmic root substance which is taken out of the quarry of the universe by the first expressions of intelligence and molded by them into ever finer and more perfect lines until finally it becomes the perfect stone for the Builder's temple.

How can emotion manifest save through form? How can mind manifest until the intricately evolved brain cells of matter have raised their organic quality to form the groundwork upon which other things may be based? All students of human nature realize that every expression of man depends upon organic quality, that in every living thing this differs, and that the fineness of this matter is the sure indication of growth—mental, physical, or spiritual.

True to the doctrines of his craft, the Entered Apprentice must beautify his temple. He must build within himself by his actions, by the power of his hand and the tools of his craft, certain qualities which make possible his initiation into the higher degrees of the spiritual lodge.

We know that the cube block is symbolic of the tomb. It is also well known that the Entered Apprentice is not capable of rolling away the stone or of transmuting it into a greater or higher thing; but it is his privilege to glorify that stone, to purify it, and to begin the great work of preparing it for the temple of his King.

Few realize that the universe is made up of individuals in various stages of development, that consequently responsibility is individual, and that everything which man wishes to gain he must himself build and maintain. If he is to use his finer bodies for the thing for which they were intended, he must treat them right, that they may be good and faithful servants in the great work that he is preparing himself to do.

The quarries represent the great powers of natural resource; they are symbolic of the practically endless field of human opportunity: they symbolize the cosmic substances from which man must gather the stones of his temple. At this stage in his growth he is privileged to gather the stones which he wishes to true during his path through the lodge, for at this point he symbolizes the youth who is choosing the work of his life. He represents the human ego who in the dawn of time gathered many blocks and cubes and broken stones from the Great Quarry. These rough and broken stones that will not fit into anything are the partially evolved powers and senses with which he labors. In the first state he must gather these things and those who have not gathered them can never true them. During the involutionary period of human consciousness, the Entered Apprentice in the Great Lodge was man, who labored with these rough blocks, seeking the tools and the power with which to true them. As he evolves down through the ages he gains the tools and cosmically passes on to the degree of Fellow Craft where he trues his ashler in harmony with the plans upon the Master's tracing board. This rough, uncut ashler has three dimensions which represent the three ruffians who at this stage are destroyers of the fourth dimensional life concealed within the ugly, ill-shaped stone.

The lost key of the Entered Apprentice is service. Why, he may not ask; when, he does not know. His work is to do, to act, to express himself in some way, constructively if possible, but destructively rather than not at all. Without action he loses his great work; without tools, which symbolize the body, he cannot act in an organized manner; consequently it is necessary to master the arts and sciences which place in his hands intelligent tools for the expression of energy. Beauty is the keynote to his ideal. With his concrete ideals he must beautify all with which he comes in contact, so that the works of his hand may be acceptable in the eyes of the Great Architect of the Universe.

His daily life, in his home, in his business, among his fellow creatures, and his realization of the fundamental unity of each with all, form the base upon which the aspiring candidate may raise a greater superstructure. In truth he must live the life, the result of which is the purification of his being, so that the finer and more attenuated forces of the higher degrees may express themselves through the fine adjustments of the receiving pole within himself. When he reaches this stage in his growth he is spiritually worthy to consider advancement into a higher degree. This advancement is not the result of election or balloting but an automatic process in which, having raised his consciousness by his life, he attunes himself to the next step above his present position. All initiations are the result of adjustments of the evolving life with the physical, emotional, and mental planes of consciousness through which it passes.

We may now consider the spiritual requirements of one who feels that he would mystically correlate himself with the great spiritual fraternity which, concealed behind the exoteric rite, forms the living, breathing power of the Entered Apprentice lodge:

1. It is absolutely necessary that an Entered Apprentice should have studied sufficiently the laws of anatomy to have at least a general idea of the physical body, for the entire degree is based upon the mystery of form. The human body is the highest manifestation of it which he is capable of analyzing; consequently he must devote himself to the study of his own being and its wondrous mysteries and complications.

2. The Entered Apprentice must realize that his body is the living temple of the living God and treat it accordingly, for when he abuses or mistreats it he breaks the sacred obligations which he must assume before he can ever hope to understand the true mysteries of the Craft. The breaking of his pact with the higher lives evolving within himself brings with it a tremendous natural penalty.

3. He must study the problems of the maintenance of bodies through food, clothing, breathing, and other necessities, as all of these are important steps in the Entered Apprentice lodge. Those who eat improperly, dress improperly, and use only about one-third of their lung capacity can never have the physical efficiency necessary for the fullest expression of their higher being.

4. He must grow physically and in the expression of concrete things. His realization of the position of man to man must be learned well at this time, and he must seek to unfold all unselfish qualities which are necessary for the harmonious working of the Mason and his fellowmen on the physical plane of nature.

5. He must seek to round out all inequalities. He can best do this by balancing his mental and physical organisms through the application and study of the seven liberal arts and sciences.

Until he is relative master of these principles on the highest plane within his own being, he cannot hope spiritually to attract to himself, through the powers of his own expression, the life-giving ray of the Fellow Craft. When he reaches this point, however, he is spiritually ready to hope for membership in a more sublime degree.

The Mason must realize that he is what his innermost motives are, and those who allow material consideration, social position, financial or business possibility, or selfish, materialistic ideals, to lead them into the Masonic Brotherhood must realize that they have automatically separated themselves from the Craft. They can never do any harm to Masonry by getting in because they cannot get in. Sitting comfortably in a seat in the lodge they may feel that they have deceived the Grand Master of the universe but when the spiritual lodge meets to carry on the true work of Masonry they are non-entitled and absent. Watch fobs, stick pins, and other material insignia do not make Masons; neither does the ritual ordain them. They are *evolved* through the self-conscious effort to live up to the highest and greatest within themselves; their lives are the insignia of their rank, greater far than any visible, tangible credential.

Bearing this thought in mind, it is possible for the unselfish, aspiring soul to become spiritually and liberally vouched for by the centers of consciousness as an Entered Apprentice. It means he has taken the first grand step on the path of personal liberation. He is now symbolized as the child with the smiling face, for with the simplicity of a child he is placing himself under the protection of his great spiritual Father, willing and glad to obey each of His demands. Having reached this point and having done the best which it was possible for him to do, he is in position to hope that the powers that be, moving in their mysterious manner, may find him worthy to take the second great step in spiritual liberation.

FRIENDSHIP

What nobler thing can any mortal be than a friend? What nobler compliment can man bestow than friendship? The bonds and ties of the life we know break easily, but through eternity one bond remains—the bond of fellowship—the fellowship of atoms, of star dust in its endless flight, of suns and worlds, of gods and men. The clasped hands of comradship of those who have come to recognize the fellowship of spirit unite in a bond eternal. Who is more desolate than the friendless one? Who is more honored than one whose virtues have given him a friend? To have a friend is good, but to be a friend is better. The noblest title ever given man, the highest title bestowed by the gods, the noblest appellation, was given when the great Jove gazed down upon Prometheus and said, "Behold, a friend of man." Who serves man serves God. This is the symbol of the fellowship of your Craft, for the plan of God is upheld by the clasped hands of friends. The bonds of relationship must pass, but the friend remains. Serve God by being a friend—a friend of the soul of man, serving his needs, lighting his steps, making smooth his way. Let the world of its own accord say of the Mason, "Behold the friend of all." Let the world say of the Lodge, "This is indeed a fraternity of brothers, comrades in spirit and in truth."

Chapter Three

THE FELLOW CRAFT

NOT only does life manifest through action on the physical plane, but, coming down from above, it manifests through emotion and the expressions of human sentiment. It is this type of energy which is taken up by the student when he starts his labors in the Fellow Craft. From youth with its smiling face he passes on to the greater responsibilities of manhood.

On the second step of the temple stands a soldier dressed in shining armor but his sword is sheathed and a book is in his hand. He is symbolic of strength, of the energy of Mars, and of the wonderful step in spiritual unfoldment which we know as Fellow Craft. Through each one of us there courses the fiery rays of human emotion, a great seething, boiling cauldron of power behind each action and expression of human energy. Like spirited horses chafing at the bit, like hounds eager for the chase, the emotional powers in man cannot be held in check, but breaking away the walls of restraint, they pour through his being in fiery, flaming expressions of dynamic energy. It is this great principle of emotion which we know as the second murderer of Hiram. It is through the perversion of human emotions that there comes into the world many of its countless sorrows, which through reaction, manifest in man's mental and physical bodies.

It is strange how the divine powers may become perverted until each expression and urge becomes a ruffian and a murderer. The divine compassion of the gods manifests in this world of form very differently than in the realms of light. Divine compassion is energized by the same influxes as mortal passions and the lusts of earth. The spiritual light rays of cosmos, the fire princes of the dawn, seeth and surge through unregenerated man as the impulses which he perverts into murder and hate. The great, ceaseless power of chaos, the seething pin-wheel spirals of never-ceasing motion, whose wild cadences are the music of the spheres, are energized by the same great power which man uses to destroy the highest and the best. The great, mystic power that sends the planets in gigantic orbits around the solar bodies, the energy which keeps each electron vibrating, spinning, and whirling, the great energy which is building the temple of God as it drives the nail and saws the plank, is now a merciless slave driver which, unmastered and un-curbed, strikes the compassionate one and sends him reeling backward into the darkness of his prison. Man does not listen to that little voice which speaks to him in ever-loving, ever-sorrowful note. This voice speaks of the peace accompanying the con-structive application of energy which he must chain if he would master the powers of creation. How long will it take King Hiram of Tyre, the warrior on the second step, symbolic of the Fellow Craft of the Cosmic Lodge, to teach mankind the lessons of self mastery? The teacher can do it only as he daily depicts the miseries which are the result of unmastered appetites. The strength of man was not made to be used destructively, but was given him that he might build a temple worthy to be the dwelling place of the Great Architect of the uni-verse. God is glorifying himself through the in-dividualized portions of himself, and is slowly teaching these individualized portions to under-stand and glorify the entire.

The day has come when Fellow Craftsmen must know and apply their knowledge that the lost key to their grade is the mastery of emotion, which places the energy of the universe at their disposal. The only way that man can ever expect to be en-trusted with great powers is by proving his ability to use them constructively and selflessly. When the Mason learns that the key to the warrior on the block is the proper application of the dynamo of living power, he has learned the mystery of his Craft. The seething, surging energies of Lucifer are in his hands and before he may step onward and upward he must prove his ability to properly apply energy. He must follow in the footsteps of his forefather, Tubal Cain, who with the mighty strength of the war god hammered his sword into a plowshare. Incessant watchfulness over thought, action, and desire is indispensable to those who wish to make progress in the unfolding of their own being, and the Fellow Craft's degree is the degree of transmutation. He must use the hand that slays to lift the suffering, while the lips given to cursing must be taught to pray. The heart that hates must learn the mystery of compassion, as the result of a deeper and more perfect understanding of man's relation to his brother. The firm, kind hand of spirit must curb the flaming powers of emotion with the iron grip of mastery. In the realization and application of these principles lies the key of the Fellow Craft.

In this degree one point of the compass is taken out from under the square. The two points of the compass, of course, symbolize the heart and mind, and with the expression of the higher emotions the heart point of the compass is liberated from the square, which is an instrument used to measure the block of matter and therefore symbolizes form.

A large percentage of the people of the world at the present time are passing through, spiritually, the degree of the Fellow Craft, with its five senses.* The sense perceptions come under the control of the emotional energies, therefore the development of the senses is necessary to the constructive expression of the Fellow Craft power. Man must realize that all the powers which his millions of years of need have earned for him have come in order that through them he may liberate more fully the prisoner within his own being. As the Fellow Craft's degree is the middle of the three, the spiritual duty of each member is to reach the point of poise or balance, which is always secured between extremes. The mastery of expression is also to be found in this degree. The key words of the Fellow Craft may be briefly defined as *compassion, poise,* and *transmutation.*

In the Fellow Craft degree is concealed the dynamo of human life. The Fellow Craft is the worker with elemental fire, which it is his duty to

*The five senses are: Hearing, seeing, feeling, smelling and tasting.

transmute into spiritual light. The heart is the center of his activity and it is while in this degree that the human side of the nature with its constructive emotions should be brought out and emphasized, but all of these expressions of the human heart must become transmuted into the emotionless compassion of the gods, who in spite of the suffering of the moment gaze down upon mankind and see that it is good.

When the candidate feels that he has reached a point where he is master of these things, and is able to manifest every energizing current and fire-flame in a constructive, balanced manner, and has spiritually lifted the heart sentiments of the mystic out of the cube of matter, he may then expect that the degree of Master Mason is not far off, and he may look forward eagerly to the time of his spiritual ordination into the higher degree. He should now study himself and realize that he cannot receive promotion into the spiritual lodge until his heart is attuned to a superior, spiritual influx from the causal planes of consciousness.

The following requirements are necessary before the student can spiritually say that he is a member of the ancient and accepted rite of the Fellow Craft:

1. The mastery of temper and emotional out-

breaks of all kinds, poise under trying conditions, kindness in the face of unkindness, and simplicity with its accompanying power: these points show that the seeker is worthy of being taught by a Fellow Craftsman.

2. The mastery of the animal energies, the curbing of passion and desire, and the control of the lower nature mark the faithful attempts on the part of the student to be worthy of the Fellow Craft.

3. The understanding and mastery of the creative forces, the consecrating of them to the unfolding of the spiritual nature, and a proper understanding of their physical application, are necessary steps at this stage of the student's growth.

4. The transmutation of personal affection into impersonal compassion shows that the Fellow Craftsman truly understands his duties and is living in a way which is worthy of his order. Personalities cannot bind the true second degree member, for having raised one point of the compass he now realizes that all personal manifestations are governed by impersonal principles.

5. At this point the candidate consecrates the five senses to the study of human problems with the unfolding of sense centers as the motive, for he realizes that the five senses are keys, the proper

application of which will give him material for spiritual transmutation if he will apply to them the common divisor of analogy.

The Entered Apprentice may be termed a materialistic degree. The Fellow Craft is religious and mystical, while the Master Mason is occult or philosophical. Each of these is a degree in the unfoldment of a connected life and intelligence, which reveals in ever greater expression the gradual liberation of the Master from the triangular cell of threefold negation which marks the early stage of individualization.

The Master Mason, whose living bodies have become the capstone of the Universal Temple. -:- -:- -:-

In this picture is concealed the allegory of the Lost Word. The Master Mason, having completed his labors, becomes a worker in a higher plan than the one in which the ordinary builder is permitted to work. -:- -:- -:- -:- -:- -:-

The Master Mason

THOUGHTLESSNESS

The most noble tool of the Mason is his mind, but its value is measured by the use made of it. Thoughtful in all things, the aspiring candidate to divine wisdom attains reality in sincere desire, in meditation, and in silence. Let the keynote of the Craft, and of the Ritual, be written in blazing letters: THINK ON ME. What is the meaning of this mystic maze of symbols, rites and rituals? Think! What does life mean, with the criss-crossings of human relationship, the endless pageantry of qualities masquerading in a carnival of fools? Think! What is the plan behind it all, and who the planner? Where dwells the Great Architect, and what is the tracing board upon which he designs? Think! What is the human soul, and why the endless yearning to ends unknown, along pathways where each must wander unaccompanied? Why mind, why soul, why spirit, and in truth, why anything? Think! Is there an answer? If so, where will the truth be found? Think, Brothers of the Craft, think deeply, for if truth exists, you have it, and if truth be within the reach of living creature, what other goal is worth the struggle?

Chapter Four

THE MASTER MASON

ON the upper step of spiritual unfoldment stands the Master Mason, who spiritually represents the graduate from the school of esoteric learning. Among the ancient symbols he is represented as an old man leaning upon a staff, his long white beard upon his chest, and his deep piercing eyes sheltered by the brows of a philosopher. He is in truth old, not in years, but in the wisdom and understanding which are the only true measurement of age. Through years and lives of labor he has found the staff of life and truth upon which he leans. He no longer depends upon the words of others but upon the still voice that speaks from the heart of his own being. There is no more glorious position that a man may hold than that of a Master Builder, who has risen by laboring through the degrees of human consciousness. Time is the differentiation of eternity constructed by man to measure the passage of human events; on the spiritual planes of nature it is the space or distance between stages of spiritual growth and is not measured by material things.

Many a child comes into this world a Grand Master of the Masonic School, while many a revered and honored brother passes silently to rest without having gained admittance to its gate. The Master Mason is one whose life is full, pressed down and brimming over with experience which he has gained in his slow pilgrimage up the winding stairs.

The Master Mason represents the power of the human mind, the connecting link which binds heaven and earth together in an endless chain. His spiritual light is greater because he has evolved a higher vehicle for its expression. Even above constructive action and emotion soars the power of thought which swiftly flies on wings to the source of Light. The mind is the highest form of his human expression and he passes into the great darkness of the inner room illuminated only by the fruits of reason. The glorious privileges of a Master Mason are in keeping with his greater knowledge and wisdom. From the student he has blossomed forth as the teacher; from the kingdom of those who follow he has joined that little group who must always lead the way. For him the Heavens have opened and the Great Light has shone down, bathing him in its radiance. The Prodigal Son, so long a wanderer in the regions of darkness, has returned again to his Father's house. The voice speaks from the Heavens, its power thrilling the Master until his own being seems filled with its divinity, saying, "This is my beloved son, in whom I am well pleased." The ancients taught that the sun was not a source of light, life, or power, but a medium through which life and light were reflected into physical substance. The Master Mason is in truth a Sun, a great reflector of light, who radiates through his organism, purified by ages of preparation, the glorious power which is the light of the Lodge. He, in truth, has become the spokesman of the Most High. He stands between the glowing fire light and the world. Through him passes Hydra, the great snake, and from its mouth there pours to man the light of God. His symbol is the rising sun, for in him the globe of day has indeed risen in all its splendor from the darkness of the night, illuminating the immortal East with the first promise of approaching day.

With a sigh the Master lays aside his tools. For him the temple is nearing completion, the last stones are being placed, and he slakes his lime with a vague regret as he sees dome and minaret rise through the power of his handiwork. The true Master does not long for rest, and as he sees the days of his labor close, a sadness weighs upon his heart. Slowly the brothers of his Craft leave him, each going his respective way; and, climbing step by step, the Master stands alone on the cap of the temple. One stone must yet be placed but this he cannot find. Somewhere it lies concealed. He kneels in prayer asking that the powers that be aid him in his search. The light of the sun shines upon him and bathes him in a splendor celestial. Suddenly a voice speaks from the Heavens, saying, "The temple is finished and in my faithful Master is found the missing stone."

Both points of the compass are now lifted from under the square. The Divine is liberated from its cube; heart and mind alike are liberated from the symbol of mortality, and as emotion and thought they unite for the glorification of the greatest and the highest. Then the Sun and Moon are united and the Hermetic Degree is consummated.

The Master Mason is presented with opportunities far beyond the reach of ordinary man, but he must not fail to realize that every opportunity brings with it a cosmic responsibility. It is worse far to know and not to do than never to have known at all. He realizes that the choice of avoiding responsibility is no longer his and that for him all problems must be met and solved. The only joy in the heart of the Master is the joy of seeing the fruits of his handiwork. It can be truly said of the Master that through suffering he has learned to be glad, through weeping he has learned to smile, and through dying he has learned to live. The purification and probationship of his previous Degrees have so spiritualized his being that he is in truth a glorious example of God's Plan for his children. The greatest sermon he can preach, the greatest lesson he can teach, is that of standing forth a living proof of the Eternal Plan. The Master Mason is not ordained: he is a natural product of cause and effect, and none but those who live the cause can produce the effect. The Master Mason, if he be truly a Master, is in communication with the unseen powers that move the destinies of life. As the Eldest Brother of the Lodge he is the spokesman for the Spiritual Hierarchies of his Craft. He no longer follows the direction of others, but on his own tracing board he lays out the plans which his brothers are to follow. He realizes this, and so lives that every line and plan which he gives out is inspired by the Divine within himself. His glorious opportunity to be a factor in the growth of others comes before all else. At the seat of mercy he kneels, a faithful servant of the Highest within himself and worthy to be given control over the lives of others by having first controlled himself.

Much is said concerning the loss of the Master's Word and how the parties go out to seek it but bring back only substitutes. The true Master knows that those who go out can never find the secret trust. He alone can find it by going within. The true Master Builder has never lost the Word but has cherished it in the spiritual locket of his own being. From those who have the eyes to see nothing is concealed; to those who have the right to know, all things are open books. The true Word of the three Grand Masters has never been concealed from those who have the right to know it nor has it ever been revealed to those who have not prepared a worthy shrine to contain it. The Master knows: he is a Shrine Builder. Within the setting of his own bodies the Philosopher's Stone is placed, for in truth it is the heart of the Phenix, that strange bird which rises with renewed youth from the ashes of its burned body. When the Master's heart is as pure and white as the diamond that he wears he will then become a living stone, the crown jewel in the diadem of his Craft.

The Word is found when the Master himself is ordained by the living hand of God, cleansed by living water, baptized by living fire, a Priest King after the Order of Melchizedek who is above the law.

THE MASTER MASON

The great work of the Master Mason can be called the art of balance. To him is given the work of balancing the triangle, that it may blaze forth with the glory of the Divine Degree. The triple energies of thought, desire, and action must be united in a harmonious blending of expression. He holds in his hands the triple keys; he wears the triple crown of the Ancient Magus for he is in truth the King of Heaven, Earth, and Hell. Salt, Sulphur, and Mercury are the elements of his work and with the philosophical Mercury he seeks to blend all powers to the glorifying of one end.

There is behind the Degree of Master Mason another, not known to earth. Far above him stretch other steps concealed by the Blue Veil which divides the seen from the unseen. The true Brother knows this, therefore he works with an end in view far above the concept of mortal mind. He seeks to be worthy to pass behind that veil and to join that band who, unhonored and unsung, carry the responsibilities of human growth. His eyes are fixed forever on the Seven Stars which shine down from somewhere above the upper rung of the ladder. With hope, faith, and charity he climbs the steps, and whispering the Master's Word to the Keeper of the Gates, passes on behind the veil. It is then, and then only, that a true Mason is born.

It is only behind this veil that the mystic student comes into his own. These things which we see around us are but forms: promises of a thing unnamed: symbols of a truth unknown. It is in the spiritual temple built without the voice of workmen or the sound of hammers that the true initiation is given, and there, robed in the simple lambskin of a purified body, the student becomes a Master Mason, chosen out of the world as ready to be an active worker in the name of the Great Architect. It is there alone, unseen by mortal eyes, that the Great Degrees are given and there the soul radiating the light of Spirit becomes a living star in the Blue Canopy of the Masonic Lodge.

The Qualifications of a True Mason

THE PRESENCE OF THE MASTER

The Mason believes in the great Architect, the living keystone of creation's plan, the Master of all Lodges, without whose spirit there is no work. Let him never forget that the Master is near. Day and night let him feel the presence of the Supreme or Shadowing One. The All-Seeing Eye is upon him. Day and night this great Orb measures his depth, seeing into the innermost soul of his souls, judging his life, reading his thought, measuring his aspiration, and rewarding his sincerity. To this all-seeing One he is accountable; to none other must he account. This Spirit passes with him out of the Lodge and measures the Mason in the world. This Spirit is with him when he buys and sells. It is with him in his home. By the light of day and by the darkness of night It judges him. It hears each thoughtless word. It is the silent witness to every transaction of life, the silent partner of every man. By the jury of his acts, each man is judged. Let every Mason know that his obligations include not only those within the narrow Lodge, bordered by walls of stone and brick, but those in the Great Lodge, walled only by the dome of heaven. The Valley of Jehoshaphat waits for him who is false to any creature, as surely as it waited for the breakers of the Cosmic oath.

Chapter Five

THE QUALIFICATIONS OF A TRUE MASON

1. All true Masons have come into the realization that there is but one Lodge and that is the Universe. There is but one Brotherhood and this is composed of everything that moves or exists in any of the planes of Nature. He realizes that the Temple of Solomon is really the Temple of the Solar Man, Sol Om On, the King of the Universe manifesting through his three primordial builders. He realizes that his vow of Brotherhood and Fraternity is universal, and that plant, animal, mineral, and man are all included in the true Masonic Craft. His duty as an elder brother to all the kingdoms of Nature beneath him is well understood by the true Craftsman, who would rather die than fail in this, his great obligation. He has dedicated his life upon the Altar of his God and is willing and glad to serve the lesser through the powers he has gained from the greater. The Mystic Mason, in building the eyes that see behind the apparent ritual, recognizes the oneness of life manifesting through the diversity of form.

2. A true disciple of Ancient Masonry has given up forever the worship of personalities. He realizes with his greater insight that all forms and their position in material affairs are of no importance to him compared to the life which is evolving within. Those who allow appearances or worldly expressions to deter them from their self-appointed tasks are failures in Masonry, for Masonry is an abstract science of spiritual unfoldment. Material prosperity is not the measure of soul growth. The true Mason realizes that behind these diverse forms there is one connected Life Principle, the Spark of God in all living things. It is this Life which he considers when measuring the worth of a brother. It is to this Life that he appeals for a recognition of Spiritual Unity. He realizes that it is the discovery of this Spark of Unity which makes him a conscious member of the Cosmic Lodge. Most of all he must learn to understand that this Divine Spark shines out as brightly from the body of a foe as it does from the dearest friend. The true Mason has learned to be divinely impersonal in thought, action, and desire.

3. The true Mason is not creed-bound. He realizes with the divine illumination of his lodge that as a Mason his religion must be universal: Christ, Buddha, or Mohammed, the name means

little, for he recognizes only the light and not the bearer. He worships at every shrine, bows before every altar, whether in temple, mosque, or cathedral, realizing with his truer understanding the oneness of all Spiritual Truth. All true Masons know that the only heathen are those who, having great ideals, do not live up to them. They know that all religions are one story told in many ways for peoples whose ideals differ but whose great purpose is in harmony with Masonic ideals. North, east, south and west stretch the diversities of human thought, and while the ideals of man apparently differ, when all is said and the crystallization of form with its false concepts is swept away, one great truth remains: all existing things are Temple Builders, laboring for a single end. No true Mason can be narrow, for his Lodge is the divine expression of all broadness. There is no place for little minds in a great work.

4. The Mason must develop the powers of observation. He must seek eternally in all expressions of Nature for the things which he has lost because he failed to work for them. He must become a student of human nature and see in those around him the unfolding and varying expressions of one connected Spiritual Intelligence. The great spiritual ritual of his lodge is played out before

him in every action of his brother man. The entire Masonic initiation is an open secret, for anyone can see it played out on the street corners of cities or in the untracked wilderness of Nature. The Mason has sworn that every day he will extract from life its message for him and build it into the Temple of his God. He seeks to learn the things which will make him of greater use in the Divine Plan, a better instrument in the hands of the Great Architect, who is laboring eternally to unfold life through the medium of living things. The Mason realizes, moreover, that his vows, taken of his own free will and accord, give him the divine opportunity of being a living tool in the hands of a Master Workman.

5. The true Master Mason enters his lodge with one thought uppermost in his mind: "How can I, as an individual, be of greater use in the universal plan? What can I do to be worthy to comprehend the mysteries which are unfolded here? How can I build the eyes to see the things which are concealed from those who lack spiritual understanding?" The true Mason is supremely *unselfish* in every expression and application of the powers that have been entrusted to him. No true Brother seeks anything for himself, but unselfishly labors for the good of all. No

By the grip of the lion's paw the spirit in man, long buried in the sepulcher of substance, is raised to life, and goes forth as a builder entitled to the wages of a Master Mason. -:-   -:-   -:-

This picture shows how the grip of the lion's paw was given in the Pyramid Mysteries. The priest wore over his head the mask of a lion. (The grip shown here has been conventionalized, as it is unlawful to picture it or to speak of it outside of a tiled lodge.) -:-   -:-   -:-   -:-   -:-   -:-

person who enters a spiritual obligation for what he can get out of it is worthy of applying for the position even of water-carrier. The true Light can come only to those who, asking nothing, gladly give all to It.

6. The true brother of the Craft, while steadily striving to improve himself, mentally, physically, and spiritually through the days of his life, never sets his own desires as the guiding star for his works. He has a duty and that duty is to fit into the Plans of Another. He must be ready at any hour of the day or night to drop his own ideals at the call of the Builder. The work must be done and he has dedicated his life to the service of those who know not the bonds of time or space. He must be ready at any moment and his life should be turned into preparing himself for that call which may come when he least expects it. The Master Mason knows that those who are of greatest use in the Plan are the ones who have gained the most from the practical experiences of life. It is not what goes on within the tiled Lodge which is the basis of his greatness, but it is the way that he meets the problems of his daily life. A true Masonic student is known by his brotherly actions and his common sense.

7. All Masons know that a broken vow brings

with it a terrible penalty. Let them also realize that failing to live mentally, spiritually, and morally up to the highest standard which they are capable of conceiving constitutes the greatest of all broken oaths. When a Mason swears that he will devote his life to the building of his Father's house and then defiles his living temple through the perversion of mental power, emotional force, and active energy, he is breaking a vow which brings with it not hours but ages of misery. If he is worthy to be a Mason he must be great enough to restrain the lower side of his own nature which is daily murdering his Grand Master. He realizes that a misdirected life is a broken vow and that daily service, purification, and the constructive application of energy is a living invocation which builds within himself and draws to him the power of the Creator. His life is the only prayer acceptable in the eyes of the Most High. An impure life is a broken trust; a destructive action is a living curse; a narrow mind is a strangle-cord around the throat of God.

8. All true Masons know that their work is not secret. They also realize that it must remain unknown to all who do not live the true Masonic life. If the secrets of Masonry were shouted from the housetops they would be absolutely safe. Certain

spiritual qualities are necessary before Masonic secrets can be understood by the Brothers themselves. It is only those who have been weighed in the balance and found true, upright, and square who have prepared themselves by their own growth to appreciate the inner meanings of their Craft. To the rest of their Brethren within or without the Lodge their sacred rituals must remain, as Shakespeare might have said, "Words, words, words." Within the Mason's own being is concealed the Power, which, blazing forth from his purified being, constiutes the Builder's Word. His life is the password which admits him to the true Masonic Lodge. His spiritual urge is the sprig of acacia which through the darkness of ignorance still proves that the spiritual fire is alight. Within himself he must build those qualities which will make possible his true understanding of the Craft. He can show the world only forms which mean nothing; the life within is forever concealed until the eye of Spirit reveals it.

9. The Master Mason realizes that charity is one of the greatest traits which the Elder Brothers have unfolded, which means not only properly regulated charity of the purse but charity in thought and action. He realizes that all the workmen are not on the same step but wherever they

may be they are doing the best they can according to their light. Each is laboring with the tools that he has, and he, as a Master Mason, does not spend his time in criticizing but in helping them to improve their tools. Instead of blaming poor tools let us always blame ourselves for having them. The Master Mason does not find fault, he does not criticize nor does he complain, but with malice toward none and charity to all he seeks to be worthy of his Father's trust. In silence he labors, with compassion he suffers, and if the builders strike him as he seeks to work with them, his last word will be a prayer for them. The greater the Mason, the more advanced in his Craft, the more fatherly he grows, the walls of his Lodge broadening out until all living things are sheltered and guarded within the blue folds of his cape. From laboring with the few he seeks to assist all, realizing with his broader understanding the weaknesses of others but the strength of right.

10. A Mason is not proud of his position. He is not puffed up by his honor, but with a sinking heart is eternally ashamed of his own place, realizing that it is far below the standard of his Craft. The farther on he goes the more he realizes that he is standing on slippery places and if he allows himself for one moment to lose his simplicity and

humility, a fall is inevitable. A true Mason never feels himself worthy of his Craft. A student may stand on the top of Fool's Mountain self-satisfied in his position, but the true brother is always notable for his simplicity.

11. A Mason cannot be ordained or elected by ballot. He is evolved through ages of self purification and spiritual transmutation. There are thousands of Masons today who are Brethren in name only, for their methods of living prevent them from receiving the slightest idea of what true Masonry teaches or means. The Masonic Life forms the first key of the Temple and without this key none of the doors can be opened. When this fact is better realized and lived, Masonry will awake, and speak the Word so long withheld. The speculative Craft will then become operative, and the Ancient Wisdom so long concealed will rise from the ruins of its temple as the greatest Spiritual Truth yet revealed to man, the Ancient and Accepted Masonic Rite.

12. The true Master Mason realizes the value of seeking for truth wherever he can find it. It makes no difference to him if it be in the enemy's camp, if it be truth, he will go there gladly to secure it. The Masonic Lodge is universal, therefore all true Masons will seek through the extremi-

ties of creation for their Light. The true brother of the Craft knows and applies one great principle. He must search for the high things in lowly places and he will always find the low things in high places. Any Mason who feels holier than his brother man has built a wall around himself through which no light can pass, for the one who in truth is the greatest is the servant of all. Many brothers make a great mistake in building a wall around their secrets, for they succeed only in shutting out their own light. Their divine opportunity is at hand. The time has come when the world needs the ancient Wisdom as never before. Let the Mason stand forth and by living the doctrines which he preaches show to his brother man the glory of his work. He holds the keys to truth; let him unlock the door, and with his life and not his words preach the doctrine which he has so long professed.

The Fatherhood of God and the Brotherhood of Man were united in the completion of the Eternal Temple, the Great Work, for which all things came into being and through which all shall glorify their Creator.

EPILOGUE

IN THE TEMPLE OF COSMOS
THE PRIEST OF RA

WHAT words are there in modern language to describe the great temple of Ammon Ra? Now it stands on the sand of Egypt a pile of broken ruins, but in the days gone by it rose a forest of plumed pillars holding up roofs of solid sandstone, carved into friezes of lotus blossoms and papyri plants by hands long still, colored lifelike by pigments the secrets of which were lost with the civilization that discovered them.

A checkerboard floor of black and white blocks stretched out until it was lost among the wilderness of pillars, and from the massive walls the faces of gods unnamed looked down in passive grandeur upon the silent files of priests that kept alight the altar fires, whose feeble glow alone lighted the massive chambers through the darkness of Egyptian night. It was a weird, impressive scene, and the flickering lights sent strange, ghastly forms scurrying among the piles of granite which rose like mighty altars from the darkness below to be lost again in the shadows above.

Suddenly a figure appeared from among the shadows, carrying in his hand a small oil lamp which cut the darkness like a little star and brought into strange relief the figure of him who bore it. He appeared to be old, for his long beard and braided hair were quite gray, but his large black eyes shone with a fire seldom seen even in youth. He was robed from head to foot in blue and gold, and around his forehead was coiled a snake of precious metal, set with jewelled eyes that gave out flashes of light when the flame struck them. Never had the light of Ra's chamber shone on a grander head or a more powerful form than that of the high priest of the temple. He was the mouthpiece of the gods and the sacred wisdom of ancient Egypt was written in fiery letters on his soul. As he crossed the great room, in one hand the sceptre of the priestcraft and in the other the tiny lamp, he was more like a spirit visitor from beyond the mountains of death than a physical being, for his jewelled sandals made no sound and the sheen from his robes formed a halo of light around his stately form.

Down through the silent passageways, lined with their massive pillars, passed the phantom form— down steps lined with kneeling sphinxes and through avenues of crouching lions the priest lighted his way until at last he reached a vaulted chamber on the marble floor of which strange designs were traced in a language long forgotten. Each angle of the many-sided and dimly-lighted room was formed by a seated figure carved in stone, so massive that its head and shoulders were lost in shadows no eye could pierce.

In the centre of this mystic chamber stood a great chest. It was of some black stone carved with serpents and strange winged dragons. The lid was a solid slab, weighing hundreds of pounds, without a handle of any kind and apparently there was no way of opening it without the use of Herculean powers.

The high priest leaned over and with the lamp he carried, lighted the fire upon an altar that stood near, sending shadows of that weird room scurrying into the distant corners. As the flame rose it was reflected from the great stone faces above, all of which seemed to stare at the black coffer in the center of the room with strange, sightless eyes.

The priest raised his serpent-wound staff and facing the chest of sombre marble called out in a voice that echoed and re-echoed from every corner of the ancient temple:

"Aradamas, come forth!"

Then a strange thing happened. The heavy slab

that formed the cover of the great ark slowly raised
as though unseen hands were lifting it, and there
arose from the dark opening a slim, white-clad
figure with his forearms crossed on his breast. It
was that of a man of perhaps thirty years, his long,
black hair hanging on his white-robed shoulders in
strange contrast to the seamless garment that he
wore. His face, devoid of emotion, was as hand-
some and immovable as the great face of Ammon
Ra that gazed down upon the scene. Silently Aradamas stepped from the ancient tomb and advanced slowly toward the high priest. When he
was about ten paces from the representative of the
gods on earth, he stopped, unfolded his arms, and
extended them across his chest in salutation. In
one hand he carried a cross with a ring as the upper
arm and this he held out to the priest. Aradamas
stood in silence as the high priest, raising his
sceptre to one of the great stone figures, began an
invocation to the Sun-God of the universe. This
finished, he addressed the youthful figure:

"Aradamas, you seek to know the mystery of
creation, you ask that the divine illumination of the
Thrice-Greatest and the wisdom that for ages has
been the one gift the gods would shower upon
mankind, be entrusted to you. Of the thing
you ask you little understand, but those who know

have said that he who proves worthy may receive the truth. Therefore, stand you here today to prove your divine birthright to the teaching that you ask."

The priest pronounced these words slowly and solemnly and then pointed with his sceptre to a great dim archway surmounted by a winged globe of gleaming gold.

"Before thee, up those steps and through those passageways, lies the path that leads to the eye of judgment and the feet of Ammon Ra. Go, and if thy heart be pure, as pure as the garment that thou wearest, and if thy motive be unselfish, thy feet shall not stumble and thy being shall be filled with light. But remember that Typhon and his hosts of death lurk in every shadow and that death is the result of failure."

Aradamas turned and again placed his arms over his breast in the sign of the cross. As he walked slowly through the somber arch, the shadows of the great unknown closed over him who had dedicated his life to the search for the eternal. The priest watched him until he was lost to sight among the massive pillars beyond the silent span that divided the living from the dead, and then slowly fell on his knees before the gigantic statue of Ra. Raising his eyes to the shadows that through the long night

concealed the face of the Sun-God, he prayed that
the youth might pass from the darkness of the
temple pillars to the light he sought.

It seemed that for a second a glow played around
the face of the enormous statue and a strange hush
of peace filled the ancient temple. The high priest
felt this, for arising, he relighted his little lamp
and walked slowly away. His little star of light
shone fainter and fainter in the distance, and finally was lost to view among the papyrus blooms
of the temple pillars. All that remained was the
dying flames on the altar, which, burning low, sent
strange flickering glows over the great stone coffer
and the twelve judges of Egyptian dead.

In the meantime Aradamas, his hands still
crossed on his breast, walked slowly onward and
upward until the last ray from the burning altar
fire was lost to view among the shadows far behind. Through years of purification he had prepared himself for the great ordeal, and with a
harmonious, purified body and a balanced mind,
he wound in and out in a mysterious way among
the pillars that loomed about him. As he walked
along there seemed to radiate from his being a
faint golden glow which brought dimly into view
the pillars as he passed them. He seemed a ghostly form amidst a grove of ancient trees.

Suddenly the pillars widened out and formed another vaulted room, dimly lit by a reddish haze. As Aradamas proceeded, there appeared around him swirling wisps of this scarlet light. First they appeared as swiftly moving clouds, but slowly they took form, and strange misty figures in flowing draperies hovered in the air and held out long swaying arms to stay his progress. Sheaths of ruddy mist twined about him and whispered soft words into his ears, while weird music, like the voice of storms and the cries of night birds, resounded through the lofty halls. Still Aradamas walked on in perfect calm and mastery, his fine, spiritual face lined with its raven locks in strange contrast to the luring, sinuous forms that gathered around and tried to stay his progress. Though strange forms beckoned from ghostly archways and soft voices pleaded, he passed steadily on his way, with but one thought in his mind:

"Lux Fiat." (Let there be light.)

The ghastly music grew louder and louder until at last it ended in a mighty roar. The very walls shook; the dancing forms swayed like flickering candle shadows, and, pleading and beckoning, vanished among the carved pillars of the temple.

As the temple walls swayed and twisted, Aradamas paused; then in slow measured step he continued his way on through the darkness, seeking eternally for some ray of light and finding always darkness deeper than before. Suddenly before him loomed another doorway, on each side of which was an obelisk of carved marble, one black and the other white. Through the doorway glowed a dim light, concealed from his eyes by a thin veil of blue silk.

Aradamas climbed a series of steps and slowly advanced to the doorway. As he did so there arose from the ground before him a swirl of lurid mists. In the faint light that it cast from itself, it twisted like some oily gas and filled the entire chamber with a sickening haze. Then out of this mist a gigantic form issued—half human, half reptile: from its bloodshot eyes issued ruddy glows of demon fire while great clawed hands reached out to enfold and crush the slender figure who confronted it. Aradamas wavered for a single instant as the horrible apparition reached forth and its size seemed to double in the iridescent fog. Then the white robed neophyte again slowly advanced, his arms still crossed on his breast. He raised his fine face, illuminated with a divine light, and advanced slowly toward the hideous specter. He reached the menacing form and for an instant it loomed over him a towering demon. Suddenly Ara-

Illuminated and sanctified to his labor by the realization of individual responsibility, the Masonic candidate goes forth to master his own lower nature— the beast that must ever stand between him and the altar of his God. -:- -:-

It is said that in the Egyptian Mysteries the forces of nature assisted the priests in their work of initiating candidates into the Sacred Degrees. These beasts and birds stood for certain attitudes and attributes in the nature of the one passing through the initiations. -:- -:- -:- -:- -:-

damas raised the cross he carried and held it up before the monster. As he did so the Crux Ansata gleamed with a wondrous golden light, which, striking the oily, lizard-like creature, seemed to dissolve it and turn every particle into golden sparks. As the last of the demon Guardians vanished under the rays of the cross, a bolt of lightning flashed through the ancient hallways, and striking the veil that hung between the obelisks, tore it straight down the center and disclosed the room beyond as being a great, vaulted chamber with a circular dome, dimly lighted by invisible lamps.

Aradamas, bearing his now flaming cross, entered the room and as though by instinct gazed upward to the lofty dome. There, floating in space, many feet above his head, was a great closed eye, surrounded by fleecy clouds and rainbow colors. Aradamas gazed long at the wonderful sight, for he knew that it was the Eye Horus, the All-Seeing Eye of the gods.

As he stood there he prayed that the will of the gods might be made known unto him and that in some way he might be found worthy to open that closed eye in the living temple of the living God.

Suddenly as he stood there gazing upward, the eyelid flickered. Slowly the great orb opened and the entire chamber was filled with a dazzling, blinding glare that seemed to burn the very stones with blazing fire and blinding light. Aradamas staggered. It seemed as if every atom of his being was torn and scorched by the strength of that glow. He instinctively closed his eyes and now he feared to open them, for in that terrific blaze of splendor it seemed that only blindness would follow his action. Little by little a strange feeling of peace and calm descended upon him and at last he dared to open his eyes. He found that the glare was gone, but that the entire chamber was alight with a soft, wondrous glow from the mighty Eye in the ceiling. He saw that the white robe he had worn had given place to one of living fire which blazed from every atom of his being as though from thousands of lesser eyes reflecting from the divine orb above. As his eyes became accustomed to the glow he saw that he was no longer alone: that he was surrounded by twelve white-robed figures who, bowing before him, held up strange insignias wrought from living gold.

As Aradamas looked, all these figures pointed, and as he followed the direction of their hands, he saw a staircase of living light that led far up into the dome and passed the Eye in the ceiling.

In one voice all of the twelve said: "Yonder lies the way of liberation."

Without a moment's hestitation, Aradamas advanced to the staircase, and with feet that seemed to barely touch the steps, he climbed upward and onward into the dawn of a great unknown. At last, after climbing many steps, he reached a doorway that was opened as he neared it and a great breath of morning air fanned his cheek and a golden glow of sunshine played among the waves of his dark hair. He stood on the top of a mighty pryramid, before him a blazing altar, and in the distance, far over the great expanse of horizon, the rolling sands of the Egyptian desert reflected the first rays of the morning sun, while the globe of day, a mass of golden fire, rose again out of the eternal East. As Aradamas stood there, a voice that seemed to descend from the very heavens chanted a strange song, and a hand, reaching out as it were from the globe of day itself, placed a snake of wrought gold on the brow of the new initiate.

"Behold Khepera! the rising sun, for as he brings the mighty globe of day out of the darkness of night, between his claws, so for thee the Sun of Spirit has risen from the darkness of night and in the name of the living God, we hail thee Priest of Ra."

A. U. M.

To The Order of De Molay

MASONS, AWAKE!

Your creed and your Craft demand the best that is in you. They demand the sanctifying of your life, the regeneration of your body, the purification of your soul, and the ordination of your spirit. Yours is the glorious opportunity; yours is the divine responsibility. Accept your task and follow in the footsteps of the Master Masons of the past, who with the flaming spirit of the Craft have illuminated the world. You have a great privilege —the privilege of illuminated labor. You may know the ends to which you work, while others must struggle in darkness. Your labors are not to be confined to the Tiled Lodge alone, for a Mason must radiate the qualities of his Craft. Its light must shine into his home and in his business, glorifying his association with his fellowmen. In the Lodge and out of the Lodge, the Mason must represent the highest fruitage of sincere endeavor.

MASONIC ASPIRATIONS
The Robe of Blue and Gold

HIDDEN in the depths of the unknown, three silent beings weave the endless thread of human fate. They are called the Sisters and are known in mythology as the Norms or Fates who incessantly twist between their fingers a tiny cord, which one day is to be woven into a living garment—the coronation robe of the priest king.

Among the mystics and philosophers of the world this garment is known under many names. To some it is the simple yellow robe of Buddhahood. By the ancient Jews it was symbolized as the robe of the high priests, the garment of Glory unto the Lord. To the Masonic brethern, it is the robe of Blue and Gold—the Star of Bethlehem— the Wedding Garment of the Spirit.

Three fates weave the threads of this living garment, and man himself is the creator of his fates. The Triple Thread of thought, action, and desire binds him when he enters into the sacred place or seeks admittance into the Tiled Lodge, but later this same cord is woven into a splendid garment the purified folds of which shroud the sacred spark of his being.

We all like to be well dressed, and robes of velvet and ermine seem to us symbols of rank and glory; but too many ermine capes have covered empty hearts: too many crowns have rested on the brows of tyrants. These symbols are earthly things and in the world of matter are too often misplaced. The true coronation robe, the garment molded after the pattern of heavenly things, the robe of glory of the Master Mason, is not of the earth, for it tells of his spiritual growth, of his deeper understanding and his consecrated life. The garments of the high priest of the tabernacle were but symbols of his own body, which, purified and transfigured, glorified the life within. The little silver bells that tinkle with never-ending music from the fringe of his vestments told with their silver note of a life harmonious, while the breastplate which rested amid the folds of the ephod reflected the gleams of heavenly truth from its many-sided gem.

There is one garment without a seam which we are told was often worn by the Masonic brothers in the days of the Essenes, when the monastery of the lowly Nazarenes rose in gloomy grandeur from the steep sides of Mt. Tabor, to be reflected in the silent waters of the Dead Sea. This one-piece garment woven without a seam is the spiral thread of human life, which, when purified by right motive and right living, becomes a tiny line of golden light, eternally weaving the purified garment of regenerated bodies. Like the white of the lambskin apron, it stands for the simple, the pure, and the harmless. These are the requirements of a Master Mason, who must give up forever the pomp and vanity of this world, and seek to weave with his own soul that simple one-piece robe which marks the Master, consecrated and consummated.

With the eyes of the mind we can still see the lowly Nazarene in his spotless robe of white—a garment no king could buy. This robe is woven by the daily actions of our lives, each expression weaving into the endless pattern a thread, black or white, according to our action and the motives which prompted them. As the Master Mason labors in accordance with his vows, he slowly weaves this spotless robe out of the transmuted efforts of his energies. It is this white robe which must be worn under the vestments of state, and its simple spotless surface sanctifies him for the robes of glory, which can be worn only over the stainless, seamless garment of his purified life.

When this moment comes and the candidate has completed his task, when he comes purified and regenerated to seek wisdom at the altar of wisdom, he is truly baptised of the fire, and its flame blazes up within himself. From him pour forth streams of light, and a great aura of multi-colored fire surrounds him with its radiance. The sacred flame of the gods has found its resting place in him, and through him renews its covenant with man. He is then truly a Freemason, a child of light. This wonderful garment, of which all earthly robes are but symbols, is built of the highest qualities of human nature, the noblest of ideals, and the greatest of aspirations. Its coming is made possible only through the purification of body and unselfish service to others, in the name of the Creator.

When the Mason has built all these powers into himself, there radiates from him a wonderful body of living fire, like that which surrounded the Master, Jesus, at the moment of transfiguration. This is the Robe of Glory. This is the garment of Blue and Gold, which, shining forth as a five-pointed star of light, heralds the birth of the Christ within. Man is then indeed a son of God, pouring out from the depthless fountains of his own being the light rays which are the life of man.

This spiritual ray, striking hearts that have long been cold, raises them from the dead. It is the living light which illuminates those still buried in the darkness of materiality. It is the power which raises by the grip of the lion's paw. It is the Great Light which seeks forever the spark of itself within all living things, and finding the solitary gleams, it reawakens dead ideals and smothered aspirations with the power of the Master's eternal word. Then the Master Mason becomes indeed the Sun in Leo, and reaching downward into the darkness of crystallization, raises the murdered Builder from the dead by the grip of the Master Mason.

As the sun awakens the seedlings in the ground, so this Son of Man glowing with the light divine pours out from his own purified being the mystic spears of redeeming light which awaken the seeds of hope and truth and nobler living in others. Discouragement and suffering too often bring down the temple and bury beneath its debris the true reason for being and the higher motives of life.

This same robe enfolding all things warms them and preserves them with its light and life, as the glorious robe of the sun—the symbol of all life—bathes and warms creation with its glow. Man is a god in the making, and on the potter's wheel he is being molded, as in the mystic myths of Egypt.

When his light shines out to lift and preserve all things, he accepts the triple crown of godhood, and joins that throng of Master Masons who in their garments of glory, the robes of Blue and Gold, are seeking to illuminate the darkness of night with the triple light of the Masonic Lodge.

Ceaselessly the Norns spin the thread of human fate. Age in and age out, upon the loom of destiny are woven the living garments of God: some are rich in glorious colors and wondrous fabrics, while others are broken and frayed before they leave the loom. All, however, are woven by those Three Sisters, thought, action, and desire, which in the hands of the ignorant build walls of mud and bricks of slime between themselves and truth; while in the hands of the pure of heart, these radiant threads are woven into raiments celestial and garments divine.

Do what we will, we cannot stop those nimble fingers which twist the threads, but we may take the thread and use it as we will. We should give these three eternal weavers only the noble and the true: then the work of their hands will be perfect. The thread they twist may be red with the blood of others, it may be dark with the uncertainties of life, but if we will to be and are true, we may restore its whiteness and weave from it the seamless garment of a perfect life. This is man's acceptable gift upon the altar of the Most High, his supreme sacrifice to the Creator.

Printed in the USA
CPSIA information can be obtained
at www.ICGtesting.com
LVHW080736021023
759855LV00005B/26